THE PHARMACISTS' GUIDE TO SELLING THEIR BUSINESS

An **ESSENTIAL EXIT PLANNING RESOURCE** for **CANADIAN INDEPENDENT PHARMACY OWNERS**

MAX BEAIRSTO AND MIKE JACZKO

The Pharmacists' Guide to Selling Their Business
© 2021 Max Beairsto and Mike Jaczko

ISBN 978-1-66782-053-8

FOREWORD:
What is in this book

We have written this guidebook to exiting a pharmacy business for several reasons, but the most important is this: over decades of advising pharmacist-owners, we have found that many if not most plan neither early enough nor thoroughly enough for the inevitable day when they will transfer ownership of their business. So this book is our attempt to help them (before they hire us!) to better understand the realities, the roadblocks and the solutions that apply to selling a pharmacy business in Canada.

This is a book for pharmacist-owners, but much of what we discuss may be relevant to many other kinds of entrepreneurs and small business owners. Pharmacy is, however, what we know best, so we will stick to that for now.

Here is what the book covers, in the broad strokes:

- Why and how to develop a pharmacy business exit strategy
- Common mistakes and key considerations in exit planning
- Why and how to hire a competent advisory team
- How to estimate – and enhance – the value of your pharmacy business

- Tax and legal considerations in selling a pharmacy business

- The importance and principles of wealth planning for your post-pharmacy life

The list of people we *could* thank for helping us write this book is too exhaustive to put in writing. We would like, however, to acknowledge the contributions of Mike Stannix, tax account extraordinaire, for his phenomenal work on Chapter 8; lawyer Peter Spence, for his insightful contributions and thoughts on our discussion of legal considerations, in Chapter 9; Joel Hall, CEO of K.J. Harrison & Partners, for letting us borrow some of his investing philosophy for Chapter 11; Sindy Jagger, also of K.J. Harrison; and Joe Chidley, who helped us translate the contents of our heads into sense on the printed page.

Our hope is that pharmacist-owners find this book to be useful, relevant and perhaps even a good read. We are always open to feedback, constructive and otherwise, so if you have any thoughts you would like to share, please feel free to contact the authors.

Happy exiting!

Mike Jaczko (mjaczko@kjharrison.com) and Max Beairsto (max@evcor.com)

All proceeds from the sale of this book are donated to the Canadian Foundation for Pharmacy (CFP) and their work in support of the profession of pharmacy.

Contents

TABLE OF CONTENTS

CHAPTER 1:

Why Listen To Us?

If you're considering selling your pharmacy, we think it is imperative that you begin preparation well ahead. We see far too many disappointed owners and resultant transactions that can be best described as missed opportunities, where significant monies are left on the table.

Invariably during this preparation phase, you will receive free advice from a plethora of people, and sometimes you'll even have asked for it. Namely, other pharmacists you know. Your lawyer. Your banker. Your spouse. Maybe your kids or your parents. Your colleague from your graduating class or the owner of a nearby community pharmacy.

The point is, everybody "knows a guy."

So you will likely encounter no end of advice, some of it good, some it bad, much of it perhaps as ill-informed as it is well-intentioned. Since you are reading this book, you're already off to a good start in trying to sort it all out. But why should you trust the advice you will find here?

The reason goes beyond the fact that the authors have collectively spent decades advising independent pharmacy owners on selling their businesses and managing the financial impact. And it's not just that we have helped hundreds of them do just that – successfully. Track record is important, and we have what we think is a solid one. But even more important is this: we understand what you're going through because we are both pharmacists ourselves, and we have both had the experience of building up and selling a pharmacy business. In essence, we are our clients.

So before we get to the nitty-gritty, allow us to share a little bit about ourselves and how we ended up in the business of helping independent pharmacy owners like you.

Mike's story

One of the things I've learned in life is that you often end up where you want to be simply by getting out of where you don't want to be. In my case, that place was the pool hall in Tillsonburg.

Let's back up a bit. My story really begins in 1956, when my parents were among hundreds of thousands of refugees fleeing the Soviet invasion of Hungary. My father and my mother, who at the time was two months pregnant with me, crossed the border into Austria under the cloak of darkness, crawling under barbed wire, in the pouring rain – the kind of scene you might get a flavour of from old spy movies. Eventually, after months of hardship in refugee camps, they found a sponsor in Canada. They settled in Tillsonburg, in southwestern Ontario, which is perhaps best-known for the Stompin' Tom Connors song whose famous refrain goes, "My back still aches when I hear that word."

Man, I know what that means. Like so many other immigrants trying to make new lives for themselves and their families in late-1950s Canada, my parents became farmers, and they basically worked their butts off over the next 50 years. All they did was work, or so it seemed to me. When winter covered the fields, they worked in the tobacco processing plant. I joined them in the fields at age 8, was driving my dad's '67 Mercury pickup at 11 and began to work a double weekend shift in the plant when I could drive myself. On the first day of school, I couldn't speak a word of English. (Some may argue that circumstance remains the same today!) I struggled in school well into high school as an awkward teen trying to find my place. The experience of being an immigrant and having no money left an indelible impression on my relationship with money. And everyone has some form of relationship with money.

To his everlasting credit, my dad always encouraged me to learn to use my head instead of my hands. That took a while to sink in, though. By the time I was a teenager, I had become a bit of a loner in the sense that I hung around different cliques but was never part of one. But I was able to collect and process information in my own mind and then communicate the synthesized solutions to the outside world.

There were a couple of pool halls in town, and some of my earliest memories were of being in a smoke-filled pool hall accompanying my dad. Later on, that led to spending my time in Anderson's pool hall when I should have been attending class. More often than not, while other kids were discovering the wonders of eskers, drumlins and border treaties in Jimmy Hart's Grade 11 geography class, I could be found at Anderson's.

And that's how I ended up becoming a pharmacist. You see, whenever the truant officer showed up at that den of iniquity – the pool hall was a veritable rogue's gallery of AWOL high-school students – I would duck out the side door and sneak into the establishment next door, which just happened to be Armstrong Bros. Drug Store. And I would usually see these two pharmacists behind the counter, plying their trade with quiet affability in their white lab coats, and I thought to myself, "I want to be one of those guys."

So, one day I went to see my guidance counselor to inquire about pharmacy school. He took one look at my marks and – I'll never forget it – said to me: "Son, you have set your sights too high. Have you ever considered becoming a plumber?"

To which I had two answers: No, I hadn't. And no, [insert expletive here].

Instead, I spent the next two years of high school cracking down on the books, and I found out something about myself: I could be a good student, and it was far more fun writing exams when you knew the answers! In two years, I went from the bottom of my class to the top. Subsequently, when I applied to pharmacy school at the University of Toronto, I got in.

A fourth-year elective in pharmacy management provided the catalyst to focus on the business of pharmacy. When I graduated in 1980, it was into a market that was far different than the one young pharmacists experience today. Basically, if you had a pulse and a degree, you had a job. Soon after I graduated, I received a call from the president of a drugstore chain, and he offered me a position. I worked behind the counter for a few years and eventually began to take on more senior roles at the corporate level. My mentors were good to me, and that is one reason why I take so much interest in helping the next generation of owners today. Along the way, I went back to school part-time and studied toward a second formal education in financial accounting.

The credentialling never ends. The universe of thought is constantly expanding, so if you stop expanding your learning, then by definition, you are going backward.

I learned the language of business, which – and this is a theme you'll hear a lot in this book – is different from the language of pharmacy. But it is important to realize that successful pharmacy business owners need to speak both languages concurrently, always in balance and harmony.

Over the years, my responsibilities grew amongst the ranks, and I became a shareholder. Putting capital at risk is scary and exciting at the same time. I had what looked to me like a clear career trajectory, founded on the belief that the company/group practice would continue to grow, and I would continue to make a contribution to the community pharmacy profession and industry. And then it all got derailed.

Sometimes, you kind of become a victim of your own success. The company had grown to the point that the younger generation of shareholders, including me, wanted to keep going, but the older generation wanted to cash out. There was a big disconnect – this is a universal force in multi-generationally owned organizations. One side saw the sale of the business as a way to reap the reward of years of hard work; the other side saw it as squandering the opportunity all those years had created. And since the senior investors owned the majority of the company, and since the junior shareholders didn't have the financial means to take over, our ambitious little drugstore chain ended up being sold to an ambitious big drugstore chain. We felt there was unfinished business. The liquidity event was seminal in that we cried all the way to the bank.

I'm not kidding – I did cry. My wife was also a shareholder in the company, and we believed in what we were doing. I can confidently say it was the single most difficult period of my professional life.

That's one of the big reasons I do what I'm doing today. I vowed back then that I was never going to let something like that happen to me again and that I would do my best to make sure others wouldn't have to go through it either. Or at least that they would be prepared in case they had to.

So after the sale, I focused on building a financial advisory practice, and I found my niche at a great wealth management firm helping pharmacists who were preparing to or had recently sold their businesses. My own liquidity event – the good parts and the bad – helped me appreciate not only what it takes to manage a seven – or eight-figure portfolio, but also the emotional identity loss and lifestyle impact that selling a business can have on pharmacy owners and their families. I just want to help people now. And I'm fortunate to be in a position where I can do it because I choose to, not because I have to.

Looking back, I wouldn't have done anything differently. My experience as a pharmacist-owner taught me a lot about risk and reward – something that many pharmacists don't think about enough. If you're not feeling some discomfort as you're evolving in business, you're not trying. You need to give yourself stretch goals and recognize the difference between working "in" the business and working "on" the business. Your goals set the course for the next mile down the road.

The fact is, failures and setbacks make you stronger in life and in business. Even though I have at times felt like I was dying in the process, good life lessons come out of that. And half of my jokes.

If an experience in life doesn't kill you, it will invariably make you stronger.

Max's story

Let me start by saying that Mike's tale of fleeing Soviet aggression, picking tobacco and playing hooky in the pool hall is definitely a hard act to follow. My life in the pharmacy business had much more home-spun beginnings. But like Mike's, the story of how I became a pharmacist involves a good deal of luck and happenstance.

I grew up in rural central Alberta into a long line of entrepreneurs. My great-grandfather got the self-starter legacy rolling when he opened a general store in Merna, Alberta, a town that isn't even there anymore. What happened was, the railroad was supposed to go through Merna, but instead it ended up being built through Sedgewick, about 25 km to the north. So my great-grandfather put the general store on the back of a trailer and hauled it to Sedgewick with a team of horses and just continued operating. Later, my grandpa took over with his brother, turned the general store into a hardware, grocery and clothing store. They even sold oil and gas back in the day. My dad decided to become an electrician and eventually founded an oilfield service and construction company.

I grew up in the oil patch, not far from where Merna used to be, where the tapwater was flammable. It was 15 miles from Sedgewick, 15 miles from Alliance, 15 miles from Lougheed – "15 miles from nowhere," as we used to say.

It wasn't all loneliness and hardship, of course. Rural Alberta in those days offered a rich social life if you knew where to find it. For my dad and his friends, that came in the form of playing music, among other things. One of my earliest memories is of my dad and his group, the Kinsmen Band – which was made up of a couple of farmers, my father the electrician, a mechanic and the local pharmacist – practising in our shop. When I was a young kid, I would hang out there often (until I was told not to).

One day, when I was likely about 6, the pharmacist encouraged me to try my hand on the drums, which, as we all know, is pretty much the coolest gig in any band. I just remember feeling so good about that, about the way he encouraged me. From that day on, I put this guy on a pedestal. (It also didn't hurt that his was the only house in town with a pool.) I figured being a pharmacist might be a career I wanted to pursue.

When I graduated from high school in 1987, I flirted with the idea of becoming an engineer. But at the time, there were probably 400 unemployed engineers in Calgary, so I decided to go to pharmacy school. This was the last year that the University of Alberta's pharmacy program admitted kids straight out of high school, so I was lucky to get in. But it didn't seem that way at first. Our first day in class, one of our professors looked at us high-school guys – there were maybe 10 of us – and told us that we were competing with people who had actual degrees and that basically we were all going to fail.

That only inspired us to prove that professor wrong, and we ganged together to double down on our studies and work really hard. In the end, almost all of us graduated on schedule.

My plan was to save up some money to buy or start up a pharmacy. I got a summer job behind the counter at a drugstore in Viking, Alberta, not far from where I grew up. I was shockingly ill-prepared, especially when it came to dealing with all the people factors pharmacists have to take into account on a day-to-day basis.

I remember in particular the day an old farmer came in and asked me, in a robust Ukrainian accent, "Where do you keep your rubbers?"

I was a little taken aback. "Well, they're right there," I said, pointing to a box of condoms on the shelf.

"No," he replied. "Where do you keep your rubbers?"

"Right there, sir," I said, pointing again to the carton on the shelf.

The farmer was looking a bit flustered, and I'm sure I was too, but then the owner pharmacist, who was much more experienced dealing with actual people, chimed in.

"Macleod's carries them," the pharmacist said, referring to the hardware store down the street.

The old fella was looking for rubber boots.

Anyway, from there, I got a full-time job at an independent pharmacy in northern Alberta, which was too remote even for me, so I went into hospital practice in the south. Eventually, I scraped together a bit of money and bought my first pharmacy in Crossfield, Alberta. It was what you might call a fixer-upper, and making ends meet was a tough row to hoe. By the end of the first year, I looked at the books and thought we weren't going to make it. I had the dream of being an independent owner, but the reality was completely different from what I had learned in school. In the real world, dreams wouldn't cut it. So I went back to my pharmacy management notes, scoured the pharmacy journals, and realized that pharmacy school hadn't taught me what I needed to know.

From that point on, I really got into pharmacy management and the business aspects of the profession. My pharmacy didn't fail as I had feared, and within a few years, we had built it up and then sold it for a tidy return. Afterward, I got a call from Katz Group, which at the time was building its empire of Rexall drugstores, and I joined as director of business development. I was there for five years, eventually becoming responsible for acquisitions in Western Canada, and I learned a lot, including valuation and finance.

I also spent enough time on the "buy" side of the industry to see that there was a desperate need for someone to help the independent pharmacy owner. Faced with the financial clout and business acumen of large chains, the independents were not operating on a level playing field when it came time to sell their businesses. In 2005, I started my own company, primarily focused on transaction advice, and later got my MBA and became a credentialled valuation analyst.

I had met Mike in 2000, and it didn't take long after I started out on my own for us to join forces since we share many of the same principles. We both believe that what pharmacy owners really need is a business valuation based on sound analysis, so they know what they are getting into when selling their business. We also see a need to help them with their personal financial management so they can plan for after the transaction, equipped with knowledge of whether the proceeds will be enough for their future goals, rather than going through the whole process and coming up short.

And we both believe that we are our client's fiduciary. We don't do double end-deals, and we never will.

So what can you learn from these riveting tales? Besides realizing that we are exceptionally interesting people, one thing you should take away is that we know what we're talking about, not just as outside "experts" but as pharmacists ourselves. We know the industry, yes, but we also know that every pharmacy is different; so is every pharmacist, their challenges, their families and their dreams.

Another lesson is that being open to possibilities and planning for the unexpected is a vital part of success. Whether you're hiding out from a truant officer, hanging out in your dad's garage or looking forward to selling your pharmacy, life can throw you plenty of curveballs. Embrace them. And prepare for them.

CHAPTER 2:

Planning Your Exit

You will probably not live forever. Deal with it.

According to a story recounted by renowned business journalist Peter C. Newman, Roy Thomson – the Canadian-born newspaper mogul – once met Soviet supreme leader Nikita Khrushchev.

This was many years ago, back in 1963. Both men were at the height of their power. On the one side, you had Thomson, the living embodiment of the self-made man – a barber's son from Toronto who had gone on to become a multimillionaire (which made him one of the world's richest people at the time, back when vast wealth could be measured in millions rather than billions). On the other side was Khrushchev, a peasant's son who, through hard work and guile, had risen to become the leader of the world's most powerful socialist state.

Symbolically, at least, it must have been quite the meeting.

As Newman tells the story, the plain-spoken Russian leader, in good Communist form, wasted no time in taking the 1st Baron Thomson of Fleet to task for his materialistic ways. He asked Thomson what good all those millions would end up doing him. After all, noted the Soviet leader, "You can't take it with you."

To which the equally plain-spoken Thomson had a ready reply: "Then I'm not going."

It's funny because it's true.

Now, we know this is not *true* in the literal sense: Roy Thomson followed every other human being who had gone before him (or would come after him) and eventually passed away, in 1974, at the fairly ripe old age of 82. And he did not take it with him: his millions passed on to his children, and the newspaper empire he founded would form the core of today's Thomson-Reuters media conglomerate.

For his part, Khrushchev was ousted the year after meeting Thomson, retired with a pension of 500 rubles (about US$25) a month, and went the way of all flesh in 1971. He didn't take "it" (such as it was) with him, either.

So why do we mention this little snippet of Cold War history? Well, what Thomson said to Khrushchev was obviously not borne out by events, but his reply is true in a deeper sense: it speaks volumes about human nature.

As a rule, human beings do not want to deal with their own mortality. They do not want to accept that someday they are going to retire, and then die, and all their worldly goods will pass on to the next generation. Just look at how many people neglect to create up-to-date wills – about 75% of Canadians, according to one recent survey. Why? Because putting their legacy in writing means thinking about dying, and nobody wants to do that.

Now, if you're reading this book, it's not because you want a philosophy lesson. But fear of "the end" is an important reality to recognize when you are running your own business – and especially when you begin to think about selling it.

We often get asked when the best time is to start getting ready to sell, and our answer is always the same: when you start the business. Yet, in our experience, pharmacy owners rarely do that. And they are not alone. According to one recent study, only about 25% of business owners have a formally planned exit strategy – and almost one in six have no plan at all.

Why the reluctance? There are a host of individual reasons, but most of them boil down to fear.

Fear of what to do next after being a builder all those hard years. Fear that they will be hit with a huge tax burden from the sale. Fear that selling their business means losing their identity. Fear of losing their equity in the investment world. Fear that they will not have enough money to retire. Fear that they do not have a capable successor. And, perhaps most importantly, fear of their own mortality.

Many entrepreneurs, pharmacists included, do not want to think about retiring because retiring typically precedes dying, and uprooting everything they have accomplished over the past 20, 30 or 40 years. They do not want to think about not going into the store every day or about the kids running the store after they are gone. We have even seen some entrepreneurs sabotage a transition for precisely that reason, though they likely would not admit it to themselves or anyone else.

We understand the fear, but it is our firm belief that the only way to conquer it is through knowledge. We will give you a good deal of that in this book. You don't know what you don't know, but we will walk you through the process of exiting your business, including what you need to get started. We will point out the things you might not know, and we will provide a set of solutions and enablers to help you avoid the trap of "waking up dead" one morning without having had a chance to explore life after your pharmacy.

Yet perhaps even more importantly, we want you to view what we have to say on these pages as a call to action. Many times, clients have come to us and all they want is a cheque. It is rarely that simple. What is clear to us, after decades in this business, is that there are a *ton* of things pharmacy owners need to do before they get cash in hand.

And the first thing they need to do is plan.

If that means confronting, rather than denying, your own mortality, then good. The fact is – and we know it might not seem this way when you are in the thick of running your business – selling your pharmacy is not the end. It is a *means* to an end.

To know what that "end" is – what their goals are and how they are going to reach them – a pharmacy owner needs to have a plan. And hope is not a plan. The most common mistakes we see when talking to pharmacist-owners are procrastination and the failure to prepare and get matters in order while they are under no pressure to sell. Then, when the time comes and the pressure is on to exit the business, these underprepared owners find themselves disadvantaged, vulnerable and at the mercy of the situation that one day abruptly confronts them.

Our goal is to help you avoid that mistake.

1. What are you so afraid of?
The fears that get in the way

We have worked with pharmacist-owners for decades now, and we have pretty much seen it all. We know that it can be extraordinarily difficult for them to look beyond the business to which they have devoted so much time, energy and money. And we know the fears that keep them awake at night when it comes to their future and the future of their business.

We understand. Yet the first step toward conquering these fears is to recognize them. So, see them. Call them by name. And then go about the business of identifying and managing those risks and building a plan that puts them to rest. The good news: none of the risks are unsolvable.

I've been a builder all these years. What do I do next?

Exiting your business can be a very scary proposition. When you sell your pharmacy, the very thing you have dedicated years of your life to building is suddenly gone – and invariably, some portion of *yourself* is gone with it. At the root, it is fear of the unknown, because many owners have not spent enough time thinking about what their definition of success will be after life as a pharmacy owner.

Is my business properly structured to minimize taxes?

About half the time, the answer is no. One of the things a good wealth advisor and/or tax accountant can do for you is ensure your business is set up to minimize the chunk of your future that the taxman (gender neutrality intended) ends up taking when you sell.

Loss of identity

It's not all about money. When you sell your pharmacy, you "lose" more than the business. What was your strength in your previous life can now become a weakness, in that you are just another person. As a pharmacist, especially in small communities, you can walk down the street and other people see more than that – they see an important member of the local healthcare or business community. If that is a big element of your sense of self-worth, selling your pharmacy can run the risk of seeming like you are selling part of your identity. More than once, we have seen former pharmacist-owners become clinically depressed after getting a seven-figure cheque.

How do I protect the equity I've worked for all my life?

Many times, when pharmacist-owners sell, they come to the uncomfortable realization that their skill set is just not suited to managing a large amount of capital. It's hard because these people are usually successful. They have built their practice and their business, they have accumulated wealth and they have successfully monetized that wealth, but now they find that the expertise required to protect their financial assets is far different. Being a successful pharmacist-owner does not mean you will be a successful wealth manager. Failing to recognize your limitations can prove to be catastrophic in retirement. The skills to *build* wealth are very different from the skills required to *preserve* wealth.

Do I have enough money to retire?

Some, perhaps many, pharmacist-owners are very affluent, and their lifestyle shows it. Often, however, the money they spend is coming out of the business – not just a regular salary or dividends, but also company cars, expensed mobile phones, and so on. When they sell, that stops. And while a seven-figure sale price might sound like a lot of money, it can burn up pretty quickly if lifestyle choices (spending) are not taken into account in a budget heading into retirement.

I don't want to face my own mortality.

In our experience, this is one of those fears our clients want to talk about the least, and it makes them almost invariably put off properly planning for the sale of their business and for their lives afterward. That is because (as we have already pointed out) doing those things involves confronting the fact that they will eventually die. And last time we checked, dying really sucks.

Who will my successor be?

Deciding what you want to happen to your store after you

THE BAD NEWS ABOUT GOODWILL

In many transactions, your involvement with the pharmacy does not end when you receive the cheque from the buyer. Goodwill is typically an element of the sale of a business, and a buyer will often want you to make good on that intangible value by staying on – sometimes even behind the counter. We have seen plenty of examples where the previous owner, still putting in time at the pharmacy, disagrees (sometimes quite vocally) with the way the new owner does business. To which the new owner's completely justifiable response might be: "Too bad!" To paraphrase Mark Twain, "You gets your money, and you takes your choice."

In some cases, the goodwill phase of your sale might last a long time. Particularly in small communities or remote locations, or if the buyer is, say, a private equity firm, an operational replacement for you is rarely available right away. That means you could be actively involved in what used to be your business for a year or maybe even two – which is another reason to choose your buyer very carefully.

sell is a big deal. Some people agonize over this. They might want to keep the business name going, perhaps bring in a younger person to take over the reins, maybe even one of their children. Others simply want to pass the business along to the highest bidder. Yet, especially in close-knit communities, it's often not that simple, because the (now-former) pharmacist has to live with their choice of successor. If they sell to a big corporation that is very bottom-line-oriented, or to a new owner who just doesn't treat customers very well, that might end up reflecting – badly – on them as members of their community. Sometimes, the way the successor runs the business is so disappointing for the past owner that they literally move away. We have seen it happen. We suspect this is one of the reasons why so many business owners end up disappointed by the sale of their business: they regret their "choice" of buyer. Of course, you need to remember that the new owner paid for the right to "screw things up" – it comes with ownership. But we recognize that it can be difficult to let go!

In short, a big step towards planning a successful business exit is to recognize and address these fears. Those who do not invariably end up planning the hard way – *after* they have sold.

2. Exit planning: Common questions (with answers!)

Q: What is exit planning?

A: *Exit planning is the process of developing a strategy to sell your ownership in your company to investors or to another company.*

Note that the exit in question can be a full liquidation of your stake in the business or simply a reduction of your holdings, but either way the primary goal is to sell at a substantial profit, obviously. On the other hand, if your business is not profitable, selling all or part of it can be a way to limit your losses.

In essence, the sale of your business is a liquidity event, where the value of your business is converted into cash. That cash can be for you, your family – and/or the taxman. As we will discuss in detail later, searching out the most tax-efficient method of selling to preserve your wealth is a critical part of the planning process.

Q: So why is planning important?

A: *In the world of business transactions, the party that is best prepared usually comes out on top.*

And the costs of not being prepared can be severe. That is the basic reason why so many entrepreneurs who sell their businesses are not satisfied with the results. According to one survey of 300 business owners who had recently completed a sale of their company, 75% did not think that it achieved their personal and financial objectives, and most said they made big mistakes and wished they could do it all again.

A solid exit strategy can help you avoid that. The benefits of a plan are many, but they all get back to this one: readiness. By that, we mean both financial and personal readiness. Financial readiness allows you to work toward seizing the full value of your business, to reduce the tax consequences of a sale, and to create appeal to investors. Personal readiness allows you to easily transfer ownership; knowing you have a robust plan will help take the headaches and the stress out of your exit. And you will be better prepared – psychologically, emotionally and financially – for the inevitable change of lifestyle that will occur after you sell.

A robust exit plan is critical to getting out of your business the way you want to. It puts you in control – no matter what happens. Think of it as insurance against a legacy of decades of hard work becoming a source of bitterness, regret and financial insecurity.

Q: Do I have to write it down?
A: Not necessarily.

An exit strategy is not a document (although writing it down is never a bad idea). It is a process. It involves – most importantly – changing your mindset from being an owner/operator whose focus is on the day-to-day (or quarter-to-quarter) to becoming a value-builder/investor whose focus is on the long term, including life after your professional career ends.

Q: When should I start?
A: Now!

You might not be adept at elevator pitches or TED-style talks, but we would like you to start thinking about business exits the way that technology entrepreneurs do. For them, exit strategies are typically core to a start-up's business plan; that is, successful tech entrepreneurs incorporate the question of "How do I get out profitably?" right from the beginning. With a well-defined exit plan, they can attract investors, hone their operations to maximize the business's value, and think strategically about what they are going to do next.

As we have already pointed out, pharmacist entrepreneurs – and you *are* an entrepreneur if you own your own pharmacy – do not do this often enough or early enough. If you are among the majority who have put off exit planning until you are actually getting close to wanting to sell, don't worry: it is never too late to start – as long as you start now.

Right away. Today. Immediately.

Q: Why the urgency?

A: One big reason is that the sale process will likely be more time-consuming than you think it will be.

Clients often ask us, "How long will it take to sell my store? Three months? Six months?" In our view, these people are asking the wrong question. The right question is this: "How long will it take to plan and execute my exit *correctly*?"

Selling your pharmacy is a far different undertaking than selling your house. You should not expect the process to be measured in months; the common idea that it can be completed in three to six months is wildly unrealistic, in our experience. Instead, it can – and should – take *years* of pre-planning to sell your business the right way, which means not only maximizing your return but also putting yourself in a position to realize your predetermined goals for life after the business. Ideally, long before the process of selling begins, an owner has worked with their professional advisors to define financial and personal goals that the transaction will help them reach.

Another good reason to plan an exit well before you make it is this: an exit plan creates a strategic lens through which you can analyze your business, its structure and its operations. In short, it gives you a path towards getting your "house" in order. That might involve renovating its corporate structure, making operational improvements to maximize revenue and profit, or assessing staff and/or family to develop a workable succession plan. Having a plan in place early allows you the time to undertake any or all of these things with a view towards maximizing the value of your pharmacy business when it does come time to sell.

In any transaction, the most common mistake we see is procrastination and the failure to get matters in order while you are under no pressure. Ignoring preparation is a huge risk, so start now.

Q: You just said it takes years to plan a business exit properly. How many years, exactly?

A: *Five.*

Of course, many exit strategies (far too many, in our opinion) are given a much shorter time from conception to execution. But to do everything you need to do to develop and execute a sound strategy, three to five (ideally) years is a good frame of reference.

Q: Oh, boy. Then I'd better get started, right?

A: *Right.*

3. Planned and unplanned exits: Beware the Four D's

When pharmacist-owners begin to think about selling, their base-case scenario for the future goes something like this: they will operate their pharmacy for a few years, successfully sell it, reap the rewards, and then either move on to the next stage of their careers (whatever that may be) or sail off into the proverbial sunset of retirement. For most of the pharmacist-owners we deal with, a comfortable, financially secure retirement is the No. 1 goal. For these people, incorporating retirement planning into an exit strategy is vital.

We would contend, however, that it is vital even in other situations, such as when the goal of the sale is simply to let the pharmacist-owner do something different professionally, but not retire. As a major liquidity event, selling your pharmacy will likely have a significant long-term impact on your personal financial situation. So even if you are in your 30s and a long way from your golden years, your exit strategy needs to incorporate plans for life after work, including how to manage the wealth you hope to monetize through the sale of your business.

Retirement can and should be viewed as the consistent long-term goal of any sound exit strategy, and it is the most common reason for pharmacist-owners to want to sell their business in the first place. Yet, in the real world, events do not always conform to our best-laid plans. Things go wrong. Marriages don't last. People get sick. They die.

This brings us to the "Four D's." These are properly seen as risks to your planned business exit because they can turn it from a voluntary act into an involuntary one -- an unplanned exit, if you will. So you need to be aware of them. To the extent possible, it also makes sense to incorporate them into your broader exit strategy.

Death

This is, of course, the show-stopper, and quite obviously we are not often in control of when (or how) it occurs. If you own a business, having a will (primary and secondary in some provinces) in place is absolutely essential, in our view. More specifically, even after your death, a robust exit strategy still has utility, in that it can provide a vital blueprint for your survivors to either keep the business on course or successfully monetize the assets.

Disability

What happens if you get in, say, a snowmobile accident, suffer a severe injury and can no longer go to work, let alone stand behind the counter? If you are struck with a disability, you might be able to manage your business, but you might not be *in* your business. As well, many owners who suffer ill health in whatever form find that they simply do not have the energy, stamina or desire to continue being involved with their business. If they already have an exit strategy, that makes it all the easier for them when and if they decide to leave.

Divorce

The dissolution of a marriage can be, and often is, a messy affair. If you and your spouse jointly own a business, it can be even more complicated. Clearly, you will want and need the advice of a competent family lawyer in the event of a divorce, but you will also very likely need to have a sound estimate of your business's value, even if you have owned it outright since before the marriage (that is, your spouse has no or a limited claim to it as a marital asset). In the case of joint ownership, there is the possibility that one of the parties will opt to buy the other out. But this often does not happen. Why? Because the value of the pharmacy is so high that neither side has the capital to buy the other out or the means or desire to take on the debt needed to do so. In such cases, a sale of the business is often unavoidable.

Disputes between shareholders

We have lots of experience in transactions that arise because of shareholder disputes. These often occur because one or several parties want to exit the business and the other shareholder or shareholders cannot or do not want to raise the capital needed to buy them out. As with similar situations in divorces, a sale transaction becomes inevitable, even if one or some of the shareholders do not want to sell.

The point is, be aware that any of these "4 D's" can derail your ultimate retirement plan and force you to either dramatically revise or advance the timeline for your exit strategy. And any of these can happen at any time. So it makes sense, when you're planning your exit, to ask yourself, "What if?" What if you die, or get divorced, or are unable to go to work? What if you and your shareholders no longer see eye-to-eye on the way you run your business, your growth strategy or your exit?

Contemplate the answers to those questions now, and you can save a lot of time and heartache for yourself and/or your loved ones should the unforeseen occur.

CHAPTER 3:

Exit Mistakes—What Not To Do

We are going to spend a lot of time in this book talking about the right way to go about planning, executing and managing your business exit. But let's take a pause for a few pages to talk about the *wrong* way.

We don't want to be overly negative – that's why this is such a short section! But we have seen these common mistakes repeated so many times that they deserve to be highlighted, explained and understood.

Often, they are the result of the fears that many entrepreneurs harbour about exiting their business. But whatever their causes, these pitfalls can not only make what should be the biggest moment of your financial life into a logistical and financial nightmare; they can also completely derail the sale of your business, squandering the potential of all that you have built over the years.

1. Implementing your transition too late

Whether it's from wishful thinking or simply a lack of experience, many, many pharmacy owners dramatically underestimate how long it will take to sell their business, and as a result they fail to get started soon enough. Ideally, the sale process – including planning – is not a five-month process, but a five-*year* process. As well, some aspects of the transaction require early attention, such as tax planning; for instance, we recommend consulting with a tax subject matter expert (lawyer or accountant) at least two years before a planned sale and ideally even earlier! Some tax mitigating strategies require that amount of time to be valid in the eyes of the Canada Revenue Agency.

Bottom line: If you don't get started soon enough, the chances of having the outcome you hope for are pretty low.

2. Retaining advisors who don't understand pharmacy

We devote a whole later chapter to picking your advisors, because it's that important. Indeed, making sure you have the right advice for your transaction (and afterward) is the critical first step in the process of selling your business, so it's crucial to get started on the right foot.

Unfortunately, we often see owners end up working with advisors who are ill-suited to the role. Many times, these advisors are not familiar with pharmacy. The typical retail pharmacist is half-businessperson, half-professional, and the industry has unique idiosyncrasies. Having advisors who know the business, who understand the industry and the profession, just makes for an easier group of advisors to engage with.

If they are not familiar with all of that, then your advisors can easily give uninformed counsel, however well-intentioned. That can make the crucial difference between a successful exit and a failed one. You can expend a lot of time training your advisors on all things pharmacy – at your expense!

3. Allowing overzealous advisors to drive your agenda

"Don't confuse me with questions because I have all the answers."

Sadly, that summarizes the attitude of too many advisors we have encountered while helping pharmacist-owners sell their business. Typically, these individuals don't live up to their own billing. In fact, the most ill-informed advisors are often the same ones who don't want to listen to other opinions, think they know everything and try to bully their client (you) into following along.

We have seen advisors nearly kill the deal because they don't know what they are doing. We have even seen them actually kill the deal outright. In a few instances, we have walked away from these situations because the advisors in question were just dead wrong and would not budge from their positions. We expect their clients got fed to the lions when it came time to transact.

Avoid at all costs any advisors who don't play well in the sandbox. Know-it-alls will cause you grief – and money.

4. Failing to engage experienced and credible experts to prepare, negotiate and transact on your behalf

Sad to say, but there are plenty of fly-by-night operators in the world of business acquisition. We often see these folks who come onto the transition team (they often want to run the whole show, by the way), and their top priority is to just get the transaction done and collect their commission. Whether the deal is the right one for their client – well, that does not seem to matter very much. And it goes without saying that if their purpose is to turn a quick buck rather than represent their client in a credible and trustworthy manner, they will not be very good at helping you.

The problem with these people isn't just that they do not really have your best interests at heart (i.e., they have *their* best interests at heart). It's also that they can undermine your credibility at the negotiating table. If you are in discussions with a large retail chain, chances are the other side will be experienced, sophisticated and armed with knowledge rather than simple incognizance. You deserve and need the same qualities from the advisors on your side of the table.

5. Allowing emotion to interfere with pragmatic decision-making

Believe us, we get that pharmacists become attached to the businesses that many have taken decades to build. But it's important in a transaction process to be able to maintain an unbiased view of your business. That's what knowledgeable advisors can help owners do.

They can also help you maintain your composure and objectivity in the heat of negotiations when emotions often get in the way of the process. When they are too close to a transaction, many owners have a hard time seeing the facts for what they are. Adrenaline can take over, and it works against rationality. A good advisor can calm you down, put you back on track and point you – and the transaction – in the right direction.

Having someone on your team who can maintain an objective view will ensure you can be part of the solution rather than part of the problem.

6. Overestimating the value of your business – and undermining realistic retirement plans

What is the most common way pharmacist-owners go about estimating how much their business is worth? Let's call it the "over-the-back-yard-fence" method. Owners talk to owners. The rumour mill gets buzzing about how much Friend X sold his pharmacy for compared with Friend Y, and by the time it rolls around to Friend Z – you! – everyone thinks they have a pretty good idea of your business's value.

Allow us to put this method behind you, because it's not a method at all – it's hearsay.

In one discussion we had with a prospective vendor, it became clear right away that he had been employing the "over-the-backyard-fence" valuation strategy. The pharmacist was convinced he could secure a big multiple on the earnings of his store because he had been asking around. But that estimate was unrealistic, and far too high for his particular business. How did we know? Well, a good advisor will have empirical, verified data about pharmacy sale prices in that region, substantiated by years of experience in pharmacy business valuation. Which valuation do you think is likely to be more accurate?

Still, we simply could not convince the owner that his idea of his business's worth was a pipe dream. We suspect that is because he desperately *wanted* the pharmacy to be worth more than it actually was. He had set up unrealistic expectations for his shop's value because he had unrealistic expectations for his retirement. Those twin misconceptions fed off each other: "If I want a certain amount of money to retire, then my store must be worth that amount of money." Ipso facto.

Sadly, reality doesn't work that way. Before you sell, you need to equip yourself with a sound, evidence – and experience-based valuation of your business. Two big benefits: first, you know what your business is worth, and you can negotiate toward that price; second, you have a good idea of how much money you will have for retirement once the sale process is complete. Then – and only then – go ahead and plan for your golden years.

Note that knowing the realistic value of your business will serve as an important input metric in your strategic wealth planning process. Read on.

7. Allowing deal fatigue to set in

Remember: time kills deals. One of the reasons is that regulations change all the time, and they can impact the value of your pharmacy business. This can result in a lower price in the deal or no deal at all. Staying on point and keeping negotiations moving quickly can help mitigate that risk. Another factor in "timing" is that some potential buyers will be willing to drag out the process as long as possible, in hopes that the seller will just get worn down. Sometimes the strategy works because when you are off your game and tired, you might be more open to accepting just any old bid, even if it's not optimal for you, rather than fight for more. This is where a good advisor can really help by keeping the purchaser's feet to the fire and making sure the transaction process moves forward rather than stalling.

8. Not planning early or not planning at all

We feel like we have already beaten this to death, but we will say it one more time just to be sure the point is absolutely clear: You need to plan your business exit, and you need to start it early.

Let us illustrate with a true story, as told by Mike:

"A few years ago, I was called on a hot August day to meet with a pharmacist, so I went to this small community and met him in the basement of his store. The lights were dim. It was cool and damp down there. And as I'm walking into what I guess you would call his office, there he sits. He is white as a ghost – literally – and he has an IV drip in his arm. He's undergoing chemotherapy, he tells me, and the prognosis is not good.

"Talk about waiting too long to plan your exit: the man was clearly dying. So, we shook hands on an arrangement where I would help him transact his store. I got his financials, arranged the help of estate lawyers, and a couple of days later, he signed his primary and secondary wills while sitting in the back of his car. I signed him to a transaction a few days later.

"The following Saturday, I was attending his funeral. So, from that first 'planning meeting' to going to his funeral, it took all of 12 days."

That's an extreme case of not planning for your exit, but we see less extreme cases all the time. Sellers often end up disappointed with the transaction simply because they hadn't planned enough, early enough. In our experience, it is the No. 1 reason business exits fail to meet the expectations of the sellers. It is also the most avoidable.

CHAPTER 4:

How To Do It The Right Way—The Fundamentals

When you are planning an exit from your pharmacy business, it is easy to get lost in the weeds. To put it plainly, you will have a lot of things to do. The tasks become much easier, however, if you can accomplish two things before you get into the thick of the transaction.

The first task – which you can begin at any stage of your career – is to correct your vision. By that, we mean that you might need to start looking at your pharmacy differently. Now, we know that there are plenty of ways to view a pharmacy business. It can be a job, a pillar of the local business community, a building, an employer, a healthcare provider, and so on. We want you to look at your pharmacy as something else: a reservoir of value.

Once you start to view it through a value lens, then many of the challenges you will face when planning an exit will not only make a lot more sense, but also be a lot easier to address.

1. The value-based life cycle of a pharmacy

There are a few familiar ways to think of the life cycle of a business. From a company-size point of view, you might think in terms of small to medium-size to large businesses. Or the cycle might be more complex, flowing from start-up to growth to diversification and acquisition to an IPO (initial public offering), for instance. The lens we like to apply when we advise pharmacist-owners is a little different because we look at the business not just as a business, but as a value – and wealth-building enterprise from the owner's point of view. After all, if you are an owner, the life cycle of your business parallels your own personal life cycle.

In this way of looking at things, the life cycle of a pharmacy has four phases.

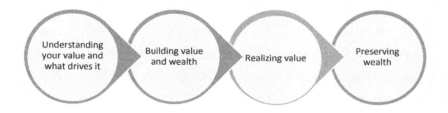

Figure 1 The four phases of the ownership spectrum

Phase 1: Understanding Value

As management guru Peter Drucker famously said, "What gets measured gets managed." You cannot go about improving the value of your pharmacy unless you have a sound benchmark from which to work. You can establish benchmarks at different phases of the ownership cycle, but it is a great idea to get accustomed to using benchmarks right from the start. This could be in the form of a formal business valuation – an independent assessment of the value of your pharmacy. Short of that, you should at least find and use the services of a reliable resource who can not only give you an ongoing sense of your business's value, but also help you understand what drives profitability and sustainability.

Remember that a big part of understanding value is understanding what is creating value. If you start off by measuring that, then you can manage it. And having a deep understanding of your pharmacy's values and its drivers can help the next person understand it as well – and be more willing to pay for it.

Phase 2: Building Value and Wealth

One day, you wake up and realize that the clouds your pharmacy has been operating under since you started up are beginning to clear. That is the day when your business has excess earnings left over after you have made your debt payments. Suddenly, you are building value and accumulating wealth. It's a good feeling, right?

Sure it is. But it raises two new challenges. The first is operational: How are you going to keep building value? You need to keep your hand on the tiller and identify ways to increase the value of your business over time.

The other challenge is financial. You might have zero-balanced your line of credit, and now you have too much cash in the business. This phase in your commercial career denotes the time when developing a strategic wealth plan becomes germane.

Phase 3: Monetizing Your Business

We are nearing the end of the life cycle of the ownership of your pharmacy business. Your primary task is to convert everything you have worked for– all that value you have created over the years – culminating in a liquidity event. We do not think of this stage as simply the transaction of selling (although that is the most significant part of it), but rather as the beginning of all the steps you need to take to realize value, your monetizing event.

As we have said before, a business owner who has not prepared for their sale stands to lose significant value in the transaction. If you identify issues and develop a plan to address them in advance, you can preserve value. Ideally, this phase of planning and executing the monetization of your business's value takes two to five years.

Phase 4: Preserving Wealth

You thought your work was done? Well, in some ways, it is. If you are retiring with the sale of your pharmacy, you will no longer be an active owner (although goodwill agreements in the transaction might mean you have to hang around for a while). Now, your goal is not to build value, nor to turn that value into wealth, but rather preserve the wealth that you have realized through the sale transaction.

The good news is you might now have a seven – or eight-figure portfolio to help you enjoy a rich and fulfilling retirement. The bad news is that preserving that wealth requires an entirely different skill set as opposed to the one you have spent decades practising and honing. Your wealth plan needs to take into account a whole plethora of considerations associated with asset allocation choices and decisions. Being tasked with the responsibility of attaining a risk-adjusted rate of return on a financial asset portfolio is no small undertaking.

Furthermore, wealth management and estate planning techniques require advanced planning and thoughtful guidance on the part of an experienced financial advisor. You might be exceptionally good at running a pharmacy, but chances are you do not know the first thing about this other stuff.

In short, you will need to get some help to protect your nest egg and attain a risk-adjusted return on the proceeds of your pharmacy business sale in your retirement.

2. From owner to investor

"The skill sets required to create wealth and live off the family business are different from the skill sets required to transition wealth, become an investor and live off those proceeds."

Remember that. Write it down. Put it on a poster and tack it to your wall if you think it will help. It is *that* important.

There is a real and critical difference between being an owner and being an ex-owner. The knowledge and skills you used to build your business are different from the ones you need to protect the assets you get from selling your business. And that matters because the biggest challenge of transitioning into retirement is making the shift from generating cash flow from your pharmacy business to generating cash flow from financial assets to support your lifestyle goals in retirement.

Pharmacy owner	Retirement
Steady cash flowing business	Volatile market
Illiquid asset & concentration risk	Liquid asset
Generates recurring income	Returns are aperiodic
Building equity & defines identity	Protecting capital

When you own a pharmacy, your business provides steady cash flow in the form of a salary or regularly paid dividends. You get some sort of return on a steady basis, and you can pretty much count on it. That all changes when you retire. As an investor, you will need to depend on a return on the proceeds of your sale, but that return is not guaranteed, and over a given time frame might not occur at all. In the investment industry, this phenomenon is referred to as "aperiodic" returns.

Every business, including a pharmacy, has its ups and downs, but they are nothing compared with the volatility of financial markets. On March 23, 2020, everyone thought the world was ending as the stock market crashed, taking down the retirement hopes of millions of people with it. Or so it seemed: the markets ended the year setting all-time highs. In nine months, then, investors went from scared as hell to extremely euphoric. That is a vastly different experience from counting receipts from your business. With your investments, not only are there no guarantees of returns, but those returns are commensurate with risk. Returns are inconsistent at best and remain directly related to the risk/return profile of the financial assets you choose to invest in.

When you own a pharmacy, your investment and the intrinsic value of your business remain illiquid until such time as you monetize (sell) the equity in your business. Many owners are unaware of the real value of their business, as it is not measured regularly. Ownership in a private business like a pharmacy also creates concentration risk ("all your eggs in one basket"); in most cases, independent pharmacy owners have the majority of their net wealth tied up in a relatively illiquid asset that provides very little market value feedback. As a result, you don't tend to think about it on a daily basis. In contrast, investment in financial assets provides instant feedback as market values fluctuate regularly, providing constant feedback – good or bad!

Pharmacy owners should consider that for every dollar of debt they pay off on a business loan, a dollar goes into their net equity. If they do well, the business's value increases every day. So owning an independent pharmacy is often a great way not only to earn an income but also to create wealth and net worth that you realize when you sell the business. In our experience, many owners seldom think about their net worth, beyond perhaps extrapolating a number from other owners' examples that might or might not bear any resemblance to reality. Anyway, whether you know how much your business is worth or not, you have some built-in protections for your equity – namely, your skills, experience and knowledge as a business owner.

When you sell, however, your equity becomes liquid, and the protections inherent in your value-building skill set are removed. Now you are a babe in the woods. That is why a strategic wealth planning process is critical, because your definition of financial success must change. You are no longer building value, but rather protecting it by managing the risks associated with relying on the aperiodic returns associated with financial assets.

3. Getting help: Coordinating professional advice

Perhaps there is a pharmacy owner out there somewhere who can competently manage through all the tasks selling their business requires, but if there is such a person – well, we have never met them.

The reality is that you will and should rely on a group of advisors to guide and inform you through the process of selling your pharmacy. So, it is important to think early on about what skill sets and qualities you will need in your advisors to ensure that they will work in an effective and collaborative manner.

We will tell you right now what the most important attribute of a good transition team member is: they must understand that they are part of a bigger picture and that everyone needs to work together for the benefit of their client – you! Failing to have an integrated advisory team can be one of the biggest failings in a business exit.

One effective way to think about this integrated team is to focus on its members' functions rather than individuals. For each of these functions, you might require a separate advisor; some advisors, however, might be able to fulfill more than one function. We will discuss individual members of your advisory team in the next chapter, but for now, let's focus on what kind of advice you need them to provide.

Integrated Approach Coordinating
Professional Advice

- Structure and compliance

  In our view, these are two separate functions. Structural advice revolves around issues such as tax planning, estate planning, risk management through the strategic use of insurance and corporate legal considerations. Compliance advice typically involves accounting, bookkeeping and tax filing.

- *Planning and investing*

  As we said before, you need good advice to help you with the transition from creating value as a business owner to preserving wealth as an investor. A qualified and competent financial advisor is a key member of your team. Ensure, however, that your wealth advisor understands the need for an objective, evidence-based valuation for your business – and that they incorporate it into your retirement planning. A financial plan that does not take into account your biggest asset is not worth the paper it is written on. We have seen several instances where a financial advisor ignored the wealth reservoir of the pharmacy business and grossly overestimated how long it would take their client to be able to retire.

- *Pharmacy business advice*
  Historically, pharmacy owners have joined in a banner program (like Pharmasave, Guardian, IDA or PharmaChoice) in hopes of receiving operational, marketing and merchandising assistance, as well as the benefits that accrue from greater purchasing power. Outside consultants might offer a more objective view, but we caution owners to carefully choose such consultants. A knowledgeable retail pharmacy consultant can assist in many areas of a drugstore operation, including human resources, operations and workflow, merchandising, marketing and loss prevention. Assisting owners benchmark their operations and creating best practices will invariably improve cash flow and create value by driving sales, building margin and increasing profitability.

- *The Advisor Quarterback*
  When it comes time to plan your business exit, it is vital that your advisory groups work together. Unfortunately, it is often the case that the respective individuals with these skill sets fail to communicate effectively, and they often end up working at cross purposes. That is all bad, and it does not serve the client's needs whatsoever. We believe so strongly in the need for advisor integration that we recommend that someone on your team should be explicitly responsible for it: the Advisor Quarterback. Ideally, it would be the pharmacy-owner themselves, but that is not always possible, as the owner often does not have the time

nor the expertise to perform this function – they have to keep the business running and firing on all cylinders. Your advisory team's Quarterback needs to be able to see the big picture – which, let's face it, can be difficult when it's your future on the line – and must be very skilled at team-building and coordination.

If performing such an important role is not your forte, find someone else to be the Quarterback. It can be an accountant, a lawyer, a consultant – it doesn't matter which team member it is, as long as a Quarterback is duly appointed and charged with the responsibility and the authority to perform this function. In short, someone needs to be in charge.

CHAPTER 5:

Your Transition Team

All babies are beautiful – to their parents. It can be the same with a business. After spending years, even decades, building their pharmacies, surviving through the hard times and celebrating the good, many owners have a difficult time seeing their "baby" for what it truly is. Because they are so close, these owners struggle to remain objective about their business – and about exiting it.

In our view, it is imperative that any pharmacist contemplating a sale retain a team of experienced, professional advisors who can help them view the business and the transaction through the broader lens of a realistic market assessment. It's not good enough to proceed based on "over the backyard fence" anecdotal hearsay. You need to make your decisions based on objective and empirical facts about your business.

Another important reason to assemble a team of advisors is that the sale of anything, by nature, is an adversarial process. One side wants a low price, the other a high price. The buyer will want you to give away much in terms of representations and warranties, and you, the seller, will wish for as few as possible. Not only do you, the seller, need someone on your side to filter the negotiating rhetoric and take your personal feelings out of it; you also need someone to navigate all the complexities, which will be beyond what you have learned operating your business through the years.

Ideally, this will be a multidisciplinary effort provided by a *team* of advisors, not just one. In the previous chapter, we talked about the several advisory functions you will need when selling your business. Now we want to talk about the individual advisors you should think about enlisting.

One solid model for an effective transition team comprises your accountant, a lawyer who understands the tax act and regulations, a financial advisor and – most importantly – an intermediary who will act as your Quarterback to ensure everyone is working together and moving in the right direction: towards the goal line. Having any one of these team members missing could damage or derail what would be an otherwise successful exit.

As a team, this set of advisors should provide you with a sense of assurance that they:

- Have experience in selling pharmacy businesses.

- Have general experience in acquiring private businesses.

- Have knowledge of or are able to research your specific market attributes.

- Can communicate well and offer effective negotiating tactics.

- Can provide well-considered and objective advice.

- Understand the taxation consequences of the transaction.

1. How to pick your transition team's Quarterback

This is the single most important member of your team – a Quarterback who will ensure that all the players are working together. This individual will represent your interests from start to finish.

In our experience, most pharmacists begin getting advice on their exit strategy by approaching their accountant. There is nothing wrong with that – your long-time accountant probably knows your business better than any other outsider. But even before you speak with your accountant, we would urge you to identify and enlist the aid of your team Quarterback. It could indeed be your accountant, but if that individual does not possess the qualities needed in this vital role, find someone else first.

What qualities should you look for in this crucial member of your team?

They should have an intimate knowledge of the pharmacy industry.

Ideally, your team lead will understand the pharmacy business as well – if not better – than you do. You need to be able to trust them, and shared knowledge and experience can go a lot way toward building that trust. Beyond that, they should be armed with objective knowledge, such as recent and similar prior transaction data. Being a previous owner – and having sold their own pharmacy – is a welcome bonus.

They should have extensive experience in many pharmacy sale transactions.

The reasons for this are self-evident, but you might be surprised how many self-styled "experts" have little specific experience in assisting pharmacist-owners.

They should be qualified.

Credentials are good – an MBA and/or certification in valuation or negotiating – but even more important are soft skills, especially the ability to actively listen. Advisors with a background in corporate law, financial accounting and tax are assets.

They should have the infrastructure to support you effectively.

One aspect of infrastructure is technical: your Quarterback should have the IT to process and protect your information, including a secure data room built for the M&A process. Another aspect is human: the lead should have a backup who is aware of the ongoing process and can step in at any point – for instance, in the case of vacation or illness.

They should represent you and only you.

Your Quarterback is looking out for your interests, not the interests of the buyer, and it's important that they act as your fiduciary and are not accepting payment in any form from the buy-side. (This can and often does happen, for instance when a real estate broker acts as chief advisor.) The Quarterback should never be willing to cross any legal or ethical lines in representing you.

*Finally, your Quarterback should be
methodical, thorough and detail-oriented.*

Your Quarterback should give you every confidence that their level of sophistication is on par with that of your potential buyers. They should be armed with an evidence-based valuation of your business before opening for sale. They should be able to describe several approaches to the sale process and describe the pros and cons of each of them.

In short, do your homework. You should be confident that the potential benefits of your Quarterback's guidance will outweigh the cost of hiring them. Remember: in the inherently adversarial dynamic of selling a business, the side with the most information – and the best preparation – wins.

2. How to choose your transition lawyer

Selling your pharmacy is not just a financial transaction, but also a legal one, and it behooves you to consult a lawyer early in the process. A good lawyer with experience in the sale of businesses is an important player on your transition team, and they will work with your team lead, accountant, tax and financial advisors to determine the structure of the deal before going to market. This is vital information for your marketing materials, as it will direct the potential buyer on putting together an offer that benefits you. As well, your lawyer will prepare and advise on the form and substance of your non-disclosure and non-compete agreements. And once an offer comes in, they will review any documentation that comes with it, such as letters of intent (LOIs) and definitive purchase agreements. Rest assured your buyer will have legal representation. So must you.

Not all lawyers are created equal, and it is important to distinguish between the different specializations – tax lawyers, estate lawyers, litigators, generalists and corporate lawyers. Here are a few things you should look for in your transition lawyer:

Experience in transactions generally, and in pharmacy transactions specifically

Pharmacy operations, valuation, and sale transactions are complex, and the Canadian retail pharmacy industry is not quite like any other, so some understanding and experience on the part of your lawyer can be enormously beneficial. You do not want to have to train your lawyer – or pay your team lead to teach them – in all things pharmacy. Usually, we prefer pharmacist-owners to work with a corporate lawyer, as they are likely to have the most relevant experience. Generalists might be fine, but only if they have a significant background in business sale transactions; you do not want yours to be their first. So ask before you hire. Check references. And reach out to your accountant or team Quarterback for recommendations.

Familiarity with local and provincial pharmacy statutes, and other specialized knowledge

Ideally, your lawyer will have knowledge of your province's and municipality's statutes governing pharmacies. They should also have a solid understanding of banner and wholesale agreements, specifically on how rights of first refusal (ROFRs) might impact your exit efforts. Leases are often an important consideration in pharmacy transactions, so experience in divesting current leases, and the ability to explain both the benefits and the obligations of them, is also essential.

Solid negotiating and interpersonal skills while being deal-centric
You want a lawyer who can play well with other lawyers and your other advisors, as they will know no doubt have lots of interaction with the other side's legal representation. Having someone capable and experienced in that back-and-forth is vital. Remember, too, that you and your team will have to negotiate more than just price; legal matters, such as the terms and conditions of a definitive agreement, require a skilled negotiator. However, we would also urge you to ensure your lawyer can keep their eye on the prize: a deal. You want them to guide you – as efficiently as possible – to a closing, not run up the bill. And always be sure to ask them for an estimate of what the final bill will be.

Creativity and risk-awareness

There is plenty of room for legal creativity in business negotiations, so try to get a sense of innovative approaches a prospective lawyer has taken in the past. As well, your lawyer should be highly attuned to real and potential risks in any deal, be able to point them out to you so you can make informed decisions, and be able to provide methods of mitigating them.

Tax knowledge

Finally, while not essential, experience in working with the Canadian Income Tax Act will be a bonus. Familiarity with the Act will increase your odds of a sale structure that reduces frictional tax costs.

3. (How to choose) your transition accountant

This section's title puts "How to choose" in parentheses because we know that it's often not applicable. We are realists. We know that in most transactions (at least those in which we have been involved), the pharmacist's regular, long-time accountant will be on the file. In many ways, that only makes sense. Why reinvent the wheel, after all? Your current accountant knows your business (hopefully) and almost certainly will know all about your books. They also know you, which is an important plus since they will be a vital member of your transition team.

And yet, to be frank, we have found that when pharmacist-owners retain their regular accountant through a sale of the business, it can be both the best of times and the worst of times. After all, a sale transaction is not like the day-to-day (or year-to-year) work of most accountants, and it can be unfamiliar territory for many of them. That can lead to hiccups in the sale process – something you want to avoid, obviously, when putting together your team.

On the other hand, we understand the desire to work with an accountant you know, who also knows you. But at the very least, we would suggest that planning for selling your business is a good opportunity to review your current accountant, their experience and their abilities.

Here are some things to think about:

Do they follow sound accounting practices?

Now, if you have kept your accountant on for a long time, we would assume the answer is a confident yes. But if it is anything less than that – if there are issues that have concerned you, but you put them on the back-burner – then the time to address them is now, before you start the sale process. If your accountant cannot or will not resolve them to your satisfaction, find another one.

Do they understand your corporate structure?

The above applies here, too. If you harbour any doubts about their understanding of your company, get them resolved or find a new accountant.

Do they have the time?

In the routine course of running your business, you and your accountant do not tend to deal with each other every day, and there is no need for them to immediately respond to you. Regular check-ins, year-end reports – most of this stuff can wait. The sale of your business is much more time-consuming, and the need for quick responses is often urgent. Make sure your accountant is aware of that need and willing to meet it.

Do they have a deep understanding of tax implications?

Just as not all pharmacists are created equal – some have additional training, such as those who are certified diabetic educators, for example – neither are all accountants. It is true that all public accountants prepare year-end statements and file tax returns, but not all of them have the specialized training needed to understand the tax implications of your upcoming liquidity event.

If they don't, get help.

So what if you want to have your long-time accountant on your transition team, but they do not have that specialized training? Here is what we suggest: Long before your sale process begins (two years or longer), your accountant should have a tax specialist review your corporate structure and provide guidance on ongoing thresholds to reduce frictional costs from your sale. Appropriate structure matters, of course, but so does the amount of money or investments you have in the company, among many other things. We have seen far too many tragic stories where even a well-designed tax plan went wrong because a tax specialist had not ensured every step was followed.

4. How to choose your financial advisor

In all likelihood, the proceeds from the sale of your pharmacy will be the largest liquidity event of your career. As a result, your financial needs will change because, to put it simply, the level of sophistication required to manage a five-figure portfolio is markedly different from what's needed for a seven-figure portfolio. As with accounting and legal resources, planning to sell your pharmacy provides an opportunity to re-evaluate your financial advice and confirm that you have the right advisor. While your net worth technically may not change, the conversion of your business assets into cash creates complexities you and your current advisor may have limited experience in managing. Your needs have changed. The financial solutions you have used in the past may not be adequate going forward.

It is important to recognize that the transition from a steady cash-flow-generating business to the income from a portfolio of financial assets is very different! Risk management becomes crucial. As we discussed earlier, you no longer will see steady cash flow from your business; your cash flow will instead be exposed to an often-volatile market. Your assets will be liquid (your portfolio) rather than largely illiquid (your business). The recurring income from your pharmacy will be replaced by aperiodic and fluctuating returns from investments. And rather than building equity, your financial challenge will be to protect your capital. Thoughtful asset allocation choices will ultimately determine your success as an investor.

Here are a few suggestions for how you can make sure you have the right financial advisor to guide you through the next phase of your life:

Check credentials

An undergraduate degree is important, but designations such as Certified Investment Manager (CIM®) or Certified Financial Analyst (CFA) suggest expertise in portfolio management. A Certified Financial Planner (CFP) will be adept at working with a portfolio manager to identify appropriate asset allocation.

Be aware of financial intermediaries

These individuals might offer advice, but their focus may be on selling financial products as a source of livelihood. Often, these advisors work at bank-owned brokerages or insurance companies extending their products into retail investments.

Find your niche

Some financial advisors specialize in certain kinds of clients and sectors. They might have particular interest and/or expertise in helping small-business owners; experience working with pharmacy owners can be a huge bonus to you – and ensure you are working with someone you can relate to.

Ask about their investment and service style

In managing portfolios, are they oriented more towards value or growth, active or passive? How much contact (and in what form – meetings, calls, written communications) do they have with their clients? Does this suit your needs?

Run a background check

Have they been the subject of a regulatory or industry-group investigation? Have they ever been convicted of a crime? (You might be surprised!) Check references and when possible speak with other clients.

Beware of market-beaters and soothsayers

No one can safely make guarantees that they can beat the market, and anyone who does may be taking risks you may not want to take. And if your advisor claims to know how much the market (or the price of gold or oil) will rise, do not believe it. Run, do not walk, away from these characters.

Find someone you can trust

A good financial advisor is someone who understands you. They are patient. They are prepared to teach you, to help you and your family beyond investing, and to meet with other of your advisors as needed. Ask yourself: Is your current advisor a good active listener?

Find a fiduciary

This is probably the most important element of a good advisor, who should pledge to act in your best interests at all times.

Consider a discretionary manager

This is especially helpful if you want to delegate day-to-day security selection. By doing so, you will free up time to enjoy your retirement – with travel, golf or other leisure activities – rather than sitting around watching the stock market.

5. A word on negotiating skills

When you get into the thick of the transaction process, your Quarterback and lawyer will end up doing a great deal of negotiating on your behalf. Being able to negotiate well (and ethically) is a valuable skill, and one that is not easily attained. It is also something you might not be able to fully ascertain in your advisors before the negotiating process begins. Nevertheless, there are some traits you can look for to get some idea of how well your sale transaction advisors will perform at the bargaining table.

There is a whole library of academic literature on what it takes to be a good negotiator, but suffice to say that some traits indicate one's potential and others impair one's ability to negotiate._For example, people with higher emotional intelligence (sometimes referred to as "EQ") can induce a positive mood state for their counterparts, and that can tend to leave them satisfied with the outcome. Not surprisingly, more favourable results are negotiated by those who have a high EQ and a high IQ.

Now, you might be thinking that making your counterparty happy is not necessarily a good thing! Yet the truth is, favourable outcomes are often win-win situations, resulting from a process described so well in the classic handbook for negotiators, *Getting to Yes*, by Roger Fisher and William Ury.

In that book, Fisher and Ury outline the hallmarks of what they call "principled negotiation," which has four distinct aspects:

Separate the people from the problem.

Emotions can run high at the negotiating table, and it is important not to take what you might hear too personally. That can be incredibly difficult when everyone is talking about the business you have spent years building. It is also possible you just do not like the folks on the other side of the table very much. Yet none of that matters. Focusing on the "problem" – which for you is, How can I secure the maximum price for my pharmacy? – instead of the people will help you clear the emotions away and stick to your agenda.

Focus on interests, not positions.

Some people hold that effective negotiation is all about taking advantage of the other side's weaknesses. That is certainly one way to try to do it, but trying to understand the other side's *incentives* is usually more effective. If you can put yourself in their shoes, you might be able to hit upon the "breakthrough" in the negotiation that will leave both sides satisfied.

Invent options for mutual gain.

Unfortunately, we have seen many negotiations go off the rails because the pharmacy owner and some of his advisors have an unmovable "number" in their head for the price of the business. Sadly, that number is often grossly inaccurate – a fact that a good negotiator on the other side can usually make plain. There is little room for stubbornness in a negotiation, but there is plenty of room for creativity. Let's say there really is a number from which you cannot budge (and which you believe to be accurate): your advisors should be able to think of creative ways to make a deal more attractive while maintaining your target price. Are there more generous covenants to put in place? A longer holdback period or perhaps an earnout? Something to be done with your lease agreement? Coming up with ways to get what you want while giving the other side what they want is at the heart of a successful negotiation.

Insist on objective criteria.

This is critical, especially in the world of pharmacy, where so many "valuations" are based on hearsay or rumour. Both sides should be able to present objective criteria for the value of the business and provide data to back it up. Getting to an agreement is far easier if you are working from a place of evidence rather than guesswork and emotion.

We will add here one more ability that Fisher and Ury mention, and we think it's something to look for in your negotiating advisors: Do they have a Plan A, a Plan B, a Plan C... all the way down to Plan Z?

Not all deals can be negotiated to an acceptable outcome, so Fisher and Ury suggest that it's important to keep a "best alternative to a negotiated agreement" – BATNA, for short – in your back pocket. Your advisors need to have alternate plans (and ideally more than one) waiting in the wings just in case your primary negotiations break down. A sale process can take anywhere from six months to years, and what looked like promising discussions last year can quickly turn sour this year. It is imperative to have alternatives simmering on the backburner.

CHAPTER 6:

Pharmacy Valuation—The Basics

"How much is it worth?"

That is probably the question we hear most often from pharmacy owners who are thinking of selling their business. On one level, of course, the answer is simple: a pharmacy is worth exactly as much as a buyer is willing to pay for it, no more and no less. But that does not help very much if you are planning for a future after a sale that has yet to occur.

There are a couple of generally accepted concepts of value, and they are worth mentioning here. *Fair market value* is the price a business would sell for on the open market under certain (usually hypothetical) conditions. Both the seller and the potential buyer are equipped with reasonable knowledge of the business; they are not motivated one way or the other to buy or sell; they have enough time to complete a transaction without affecting what they are willing pay or take for it; they are acting in their own best interests. Of course, those conditions do not always apply in the real world, so in some ways, the fair market value reflects an "ideal" price for a business.

Strategic value, on the other hand, takes into account a buyer's particular motivations in considering acquiring an asset – reasons the buyer might want to purchase this store over others. Strategic considerations might include removing a competitor from the market, blocking a stronger competitor from coming to market, realizing operational synergies, or any number of other considerations that can enhance (or lower) the price the buyer is willing to pay for a business.

Since strategic value is largely in the eyes of the buyer, pharmacist-owners considering their exit rarely have good visibility into it when planning their exit. For that reason, the goal is to come up with a reliable assessment of fair market value.

We have a preferred approach to estimating that, and we will discuss it in detail shortly. But first, let us acknowledge that it has one significant downside: in the real world, very few pharmacists use it. Instead, when faced with the inherent uncertainty of determining their pharmacy's value, many pharmacist-owners will turn to rules-of-thumb.

We like to give these a handy acronym: "ROTs." That pretty much sums up our view, because these analyses can be ROTten in a number of ways.

1. The trouble with ROTs

It is true that if you just want a ballpark estimate of value, then some of these rules-of-thumb will work in some circumstances. The trouble is, you do not really know if the values they come up with are accurate or not. They can be grossly off-base. Sometimes they work, but most of the time they do not.

Let's see why by looking at four of the most common.

Dollars per script

This is a favourite subject for pharmacists talking to each other at industry conferences. The formula is simple. You take your pharmacy's average prescription value, multiply it by the number of prescriptions filled in a year, and presto – there is your pharmacy's value. So if every script you fill annually is worth an average of $10, and you fill 10,000 prescriptions in a year, then your pharmacy is worth $100,000; if each script is $40 on average, and fill 100,000 a year, then it is worth $4 million.

The trouble with this method is that there are so many different factors that affect different pharmacies. For instance, a clinic pharmacy might generate minimal revenue from front-of-store sales, while at a neighbourhood store, those non-prescription sales might be a big chunk of earnings. Just multiplying scripts by average dollars per script does not take those differences into account. This method may be, by far, the worst ROT.

Gross earnings

Like dollars per script, this one has the "benefit" of simplicity. Basically, it applies a one-time multiplier to revenue. So if your pharmacy has $2 million in revenue, it is worth $2 million. Hopefully, you can see the several problems with this approach, as it fails to account for any notion of risk, margins or operating efficiencies, among several other factors. For instance, biologics are expensive, but margins for the pharmacy are low. If you fill a lot of biologics prescriptions and were to apply a gross earnings valuation model, you will dramatically overestimate the pharmacy's value.

Word-of-mouth multiples

This is arguably a sounder approach than the first two, but still presents problems. Basically, to derive a number for value, you take your annual cash flow (often expressed as earnings before interest, tax, depreciation and amortization, or EBITDA) and multiply it by a supposedly "industry-standard" factor. So if your pharmacy's cash flow is $100,000 a year, and you apply a multiple of 5 (which you heard was the standard these days from a peer, for example), then your business is worth $500,000.

The challenge with this method is that the resulting value is only as sound as the multiple you apply, and that can vary dramatically from region to region, community to community, and even store to store. The multiple appropriate to a pharmacy in rural Alberta could be far different from that applicable to a pharmacy in downtown Toronto. To get an accurate multiple, you need a solid understanding of the risks associated with the asset (we talk about risk rate below) and a solid base of comparators – similar pharmacies in similar locations with similar opportunities and risks. Few if any pharmacists have such resources, and multiples arrived at by word-of-mouth are not accurate substitutes.

Tangibles + intangibles

One way of thinking about a business is that it is made up of tangible and intangible assets. The tangible stuff is, well, *stuff* – inventory and other physical assets. But of course, your pharmacy's value is about more than that and includes a whole lot of intangible, non-physical things, like customer loyalty, staff expertise, brand value and so on. These intangibles fall into the category of goodwill, and so if you add up the value of your business's physical assets and its goodwill, then you will get a number for its value, right?

Well, yes, sort of. Adding assets and goodwill will indeed come up with a number for value, but it is a somewhat mystical formula. The problem is that goodwill is, at root, only a math equation. It is calculated by taking what is tangible, measuring its value, and then subtracting that value from the total value of the business. Whatever is left over – all the things you cannot really measure – is the value of goodwill. So yes, "assets plus goodwill" does equal value, but you can derive goodwill only by knowing the value first. In short, calculating value this way presupposes the value of your business, which is sort of going about it the wrong way around.

2. A better way: The income method

Pharmacists can think about their pharmacies in different ways – as the place they go to work every day, as a vital service provider to their communities, as a generator of income and financial security for their families, and so on. But when we begin to think about the value of a pharmacy, we prefer to be a little more mercenary.

We think of a pharmacy as an *investment*. And as with any investment, there are three basic qualities a buyer will look for:

- It should increase in value over time.

- It should generate consistent revenue.

- When it comes time to sell, it must be liquid. (That is, there must be a market for it.)

Chances are that most pharmacies satisfy those three conditions. But while these criteria are good barometers for whether an investment has *good* value (and will therefore likely be attractive to a buyer), they do not tell us what the value actually is.

To get a better handle on that, we need to get a little more mathematical, and luckily it is not that complicated. The value of any investment – whether a stock, a piece of real estate, or a pharmacy – can be calculated by dividing the income or cash flow it produces by its rate of risk (or rate of return).

Here is the simple formula:

$$Value = Income/Risk\ rate$$

This is what is known as the income method of valuation, and it has several advantages over the ROTs discussed above:

- It capitalizes earnings, which are measurable, and in that way is more objective than many rules-of-thumb. There is subjectivity, however, in the number used for risk rate or rate of return, but there are measurable factors to consider in developing a risk assessment.

- It is relatively simple.

- The value derived from the income method captures both tangible assets and goodwill, so it represents the total value of the business.

- It provides an instructive template for thinking about ways to grow value because both factors – income and risk rate – can, to a certain extent, be managed. As we will discuss further, improving cash flow and/or mitigating risk can help increase the value of your pharmacy and, ultimately, its sale price.

What is the risk rate?

The idea of risk rate might seem fuzzy, but one way to think about it is as the expected rate of return. They are the same thing. Buyers will generally be satisfied with a lower return on their investment if it carries less risk; conversely, they demand higher rates of return from higher-risk investments. Two pharmacies might have the same average annual cash flow, but different levels of risk attached to their businesses. For instance, the first might rely heavily on a single customer or have a history of volatile sales from one year to another. The second might have a record of steady earnings and a diversified customer base. To compensate for the extra risk, a buyer would demand a higher rate of return from the first pharmacy than the second one. That means the value of the first pharmacy would be *lower* as the denominator in the value formula would be higher.

If you apply this method with rigorous assessments of risk, then a multiple of earnings becomes a relevant tool. It is simply the inverse of the risk rate.

Earnings multiple = 1/Risk rate

For example, if we apply a risk rate of 25% to any given business's cash flow, we will derive an earnings multiple of 4; if the risk rate is 10%, then the multiple is 10 – and the business is more valuable.

Measuring cash flow or income

On the surface, cash flow or income might seem a less nebulous concept than risk; after all, money in and out is directly measurable. The tricky part is in *how* you take the various earnings and expenditures and apply them to generate an accurate figure. There are several metrics used by evaluators: after-tax net profit, after-tax cash flow, after-tax normalized cash flow, earnings before interest and taxes (EBIT), earnings before interest, taxes, depreciation and amortization (EBITDA), and normalized EBITDA. We do not need to get into the details of each one here, as in many cases EBITDA provides one of the simpler and more useful metrics to gauge a business's liquidity.

EBITDA is not perfect, however, because some of the factors it excludes can be very germane to a business's value. For instance, it does not consider differences in tax rates in different jurisdictions, which can be especially important if pharmacies are owned across jurisdictions. Since it excludes depreciation, it ignores the fact that assets will need to be replaced, and it does not account for changes in working capital needs. Given the factors it misses, EBITDA can magically make a business that loses money look like it is profitable.

On the other hand, EBITDA's benefits often outweigh its weaknesses. For one thing, it is commonly used by buyers and investors, so it allows them to easily compare valuations from business to business. In many cases, the variables it eliminates are just unhelpful to a useful valuation, as they can be unique for every business; EBITDA provides a strict illustration of operating performance. Finally, it is simple to calculate (if the business's financial records are accurate!) and it is reliable, enabling investors to focus on a company's baseline profitability.

One important note: it is important that an owner, when going through the process of valuing their pharmacy, normalizes its profitability over time, however they measure it. Buyers will want to see not just strong cash flow, but strong *recurring* cash flow. To show that, we remove any onetime expenses that are unlikely to occur, add back discretionary spending or personal expenses, add back actual wages and then subtract market-based wages. This calculation can be fairly complex, so pharmacist-owners will often enlist the services of a professional valuator to get a better handle on normalized profits, which can put an owner on the right road to determining what their pharmacy's value really is.

It is important to note that identifying and quantifying the relevant line-item elements on your income statement poses the "secret sauce" for valuators today. Without firsthand experience assessing the myriad of potential adjustments (like Pan-Canadian adjustments and, more recently, the economic effects of COVID), conclusions about normalized cash flow can lead to unrealistic calculations.

3. Applying the Income Method: The Case of the Magic Box

We will often bring this comparison up when a client starts to discuss the value of their recent renovation or overpriced technology upgrade. It demonstrates how a business's inherent value isn't necessarily tied to what something looks like or what you have spent to make the business tick.

Let's pretend that one fabulous day, a mysterious box appears in your living room. On the outside, it is black, featureless, opaque – you cannot see what is inside of it. Your children think it's ugly, but your spouse rather likes its muscular minimalism, and its esthetic qualities (not to mention its sudden appearance in your living room) lead to lively discussions around the dinner table.

But the box is more than a conversation piece because it has a special talent: it shoots out $100 bills once an hour, every hour, 24 hours a day. That is some box! Over time, you find that it will make weird noises if you do not keep it clean and put a touch of oil on its corner a couple times a year. But other than that, it keeps doing its job, day in and day out.

So do you really care what it looks like? Do you care what is inside it or how it works? Nope. As long as you are counting cash, you are not going to argue with it. You are not going to try to pry it open to look inside. (It's magic, so that probably wouldn't work anyway!) No, you are just going to coddle it, care for it, and collect those $100 bills.

Years go by. You are very wealthy. And then a day comes along when you begin to wonder if maybe you have had enough of this wondrous device. There is nothing wrong with the box, really – it's working fine – but your family is a little bored with collecting all those $100 bills, and it takes up a lot of space in your living room. Home security is becoming a bit of an issue, you are out of oil and don't feel like going to the hardware store, and you would really rather be out golfing than worrying about the thing. In moments of honest self-reflection, you feel it's time to move on with your life – without the magic box.

So you start to think about selling it. And you ask yourself: "How much is it worth?"

Well, let us apply the Income Method and see what we come up with.

The magic box pumps out $2400 a day, which adds up to $876,000 a year. Maintenance costs (a few drops of oil, some dust rags) are basically zero. On the other hand, you do have to count the money, which takes an hour every day, so let us assign a value to your time of $100 an hour, or $36,500 a year. That gives you a cash flow of $839,500 a year. A buyer, however, would probably not use such highly skilled (and expensive) labour to collect the bills, so a more reasonable market wage might be $25 an hour, or $9,125 a year. So let us assume the box's normalized annual cash flow for a buyer would be a bit higher, at $866,875.

Ok, so there is your cash flow. That's the easy part. Now you have to figure out the risk rate. You might think it would be zero, given how reliable the box is, but it is not. Any buyer would have to take into account inflation: as the price of everything goes up, the value of the money the box spits out goes down. So assume an expected long-term inflation rate – let's say 2.5%. And just to be on the safe side, you will factor in the ridiculously small chance that the box will break down, even though it has been running for years without a hitch – perhaps a 1% risk. Add inflation risk to breakdown risk, and you get a risk rate of 3.5%.

Now we can just apply some simple math:

If Value = Income/Risk rate
And Income = $866,875 and Risk rate = 3.5%
Then Value = $866,875/0.035 = $24,767,857

You could do the same calculation by applying a multiple of earnings, derived by dividing 1 by the risk rate.

If Value = Income X 1/Risk rate
And Income = $866,875 and Earnings multiple = 1/.035
Then Value = $866,875 X 28.57 = $24,767,857

Either way you slice it, you now know that your magic money machine can be valued at close to $25 million, according to the income method.

The point of the magic box story is to show not just how a hypothetical application of the income method of valuation works, but also how it doesn't matter what you spent to build your pharmacy (or, to a certain extent – what it looks like). What matters is annual profit and the amount of risk associated with maintaining those cash flows at the time of sale. Also, when considering your investment, your pharmacy, think about this analogy when considering capital reinvestment. Is your reinvestment going to result in either additional profits or simply to maintain current profits? If neither is the case, it may not be worth the expense.

CHAPTER 7:

Maximizing Your Pharmacy's Value

Sadly, a pharmacy is not a magic box that continually spits out cash. Most pharmacist-owners begin their entrepreneurial journey deep in debt, and then they go on to pour sweat equity into their businesses for years before they can turn a profit and begin to enjoy the fruits of their labours. Then, when it comes time to sell, pharmacist-owners are often disappointed in the reward they get for all the decades of sweat, tears and capital they have devoted to their businesses.

It does not have to be that way. In the previous chapter, we encouraged thinking of your pharmacy business *primarily* as an investment, and to consider its value the way that an investor would for any other kind of business asset. When you adopt that frame of mind, you increase the likelihood that the effort and resources you put into your pharmacy business are not just to keep the lights on, but also to build its value over time.

The point: the activities a pharmacy owner engages in to drive profitability/lower risk and drive cash flow over the short-term are ultimately the very SAME activities that will make the business worth more in the long run.

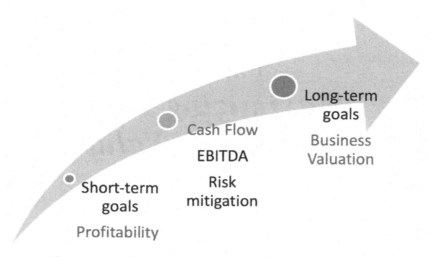

The process – from getting to profitability to generating cash flow to monetizing the value of your business – can seem like an uphill battle, particularly given market and regulatory forces that are eroding the financial position of pharmacies in general. Yet that reality makes the strategic application of best business practices only more important.

1. The pharmacy landscape today: value erosion

The only thing that remains a constant in business is change.

Back in the old days (that is, just a few years ago), Canadian pharmacies enjoyed robust sources of revenue and relatively low-risk profiles, which (like our magic box in the preceding chapter) helped to increase their value to buyers. Pharmacist-owners enjoyed a strong source of recurring revenue in the form of prescriptions, many of which functioned according to the subscription model: your customer bought the medication, metabolized it, then came back to you for more. Meanwhile, professional and advertising allowances helped support revenue/margins, and the wages you had to pay front-of-store and support staff were relatively low. From a risk perspective, competition was low – there were relatively few pharmacists and even fewer pharmacies. All these business advantages meant that pharmacies were high-value enterprises.

In recent years, however, the industry has encountered several headwinds that can concurrently depress cash flow and increase risk – eroding value. Let's look at some of these value erosion trends:

- *Generic cost base*
  As a result of the failure of the retail pharmacy industry to raise dispensing/professional fees to keep up with inflation, many pharmacist-owners chose to accept other forms of sustenance from the Canadian generic industry. The long-term trend in Canada remains that the federal-provincial pharmaceutical bodies are working to lower generic drug prices under the guise of making them more "cost-effective." In 2018, for instance, the Pan-Canadian Pharmaceutical Alliance negotiated a sharp price cut for generics. That was perhaps good for drug plan sponsors and cash-paying patients, but the effect on pharmacy profitability was a double whammy. On the one hand, it cut into professional allowances associated with generics; on the other, it undermined recurring revenue because a portion of the prescription fee pharmacies charge is markup, so lower-priced generics translated into lower margins for the pharmacy. Pharmacists have attempted to make up for that deficit by offering more professional services, but that is not recurring revenue – professional services are delivered in real time by a pharmacist, so unless you are putting in the hours, you are not generating revenue.

- *Increased competition*

  Decades-long pharmacist shortages have been offset by increased pharmacist graduate counts across the country. At the same time, the rise of international credential recognition is an important public policy benefit, but it has further increased the supply of pharmacists. Many of these new pharmacists continue to establish new practices and continue to drive the demand to purchase existing pharmacies. The result is that there are a lot more pharmacists and a lot more pharmacies today than a decade ago, resulting in heightened competition across the country.

- *Wage Inflation*

  In 2021, minimum wages increased in every Canadian jurisdiction except Alberta, which already had the highest minimum wage of any province, at $15 an hour. That followed the nearly 30% increase in 2018 in Ontario, the country's most populous province, which saw staff costs for some pharmacies increase by tens or even hundreds of thousands of dollars in a year. Given governmental focus on income inequality and poverty, we expect the trend of increasing minimum wages to continue – which translates into higher wages in general. After all, a rising tide lifts all boats. (Canadian-born economist David Card, who recently won the Nobel prize in economics, did a great deal of work substantiating this.) Ironically, however, we see pharmacist hourly wage rates soften and rolled back in some urban marketplaces.

- *Frequency of dispensing*

  In an effort to combat fraud and medication abuse, several

jurisdictions have tightened the rules governing how frequently pharmacies can fill a prescription. In the past, if a pharmacy had a patient who might have been on potentially dangerous medications or made frequent changes to their prescriptions, it might fill a compliance pack and bill to the patient's insurance company once a week, meaning it would earn a dispensing fee on that patient 52 times a year. Today, there are limitations on the dispensing frequency – for instance, our same hypothetical patient might be allowed to fill a prescription only once every two weeks rather than every week. For the pharmacy, revenue from that patient has been effectively cut in half.

- *Continued downward pressure on dispensing fees*
  Government drug plans and non-government insurers have targeted dispensing fees as being ripe for cost reductions. Although fees have increased in most provinces over the past few years, they are not keeping up with inflation. In other words, pharmacies are earning a lower real margin from fees than they did in the past.

2. Maximizing the value of your pharmacy

The value erosion we have seen over the past few years makes it even more crucial that pharmacist-owners take the steps needed to maintain and improve the value of their businesses – especially in the years leading up to a planned sale.

Let's go back to our value formula, Value = Cash flow/Risk rate. If you remember your grade-school math class, you will recall that increasing the numerator or decreasing the denominator of any fraction will result in a bigger number. So, if you want to make your business more valuable, there are two basic ways to do it: increase its profits and/or mitigate (lower) its risk.

Of course, that might seem more easily said than done. But in our experience, pharmacy operations often present some clear areas that, with some focus, commitment and effort, can be improved to help boost the pharmacy's value. We call these areas "value drivers," and the benefit of addressing them is two-fold. The first part is that if you pay attention to the factors that improve the cash flow of your business, you will make more money. The second part is that when you decide to sell, your business will have a lower risk premium attached to it and will be worth more.

Think of a value driver as a part of the "valuation two-step," one that either reduces the risk associated with owning the pharmacy or enhances the prospect of generating more cash – and sometimes it will do both. Of course, these drivers can work the other way, too: if they are not properly managed (or not managed at all), your pharmacy might be losing cash flow and/or increasing its risk profile. The better your pharmacy business scores in these areas, the greater the probability that it will garner more interest and a higher sale price when you go to sell it.

Value Driver 1: Operating efficiency

Everything you have worked for boils down to how much cash flow your pharmacy business generates year-over-year on a predictable basis. All forms of investors, including would-be pharmacy buyers, like to see predictability. It reduces risk and uncertainty. A predictable pattern will garner a premium price when selling. It is all about risk.

The lower the risk of losing the cash flow in a transfer of ownership, the more a buyer is prepared to pay.

But how do you get that predictable and substantial cash flow? Improve your business's operating efficiency. And to do that effectively, you need to measure where you stand, benchmark performance against yourself or relevant peers, and then identify areas where you can do better. To paraphrase management guru Peter Drucker: If you are not measuring it, you are not managing it.

Below are a few areas that are well worth measuring:

- *Cash flow as a percentage of revenue:* This is not necessarily reported in standard year-end financial statements, but we recommend owners keep track of their operating efficiency by looking at their cash flow – the cash generated from operations, minus the business's operating expenses – as a percentage of top-line revenue. It can give you a good benchmark for the impact of future efficiencies and other business improvements. (Note that EBITDA is different from normalized EBITDA!)

- *Professional services revenue as a percentage of retail prescription revenue:* This metric can help you understand the relationship/balance between your prescription business and professional services. If it is low, you might decide to devote more resources to drive services; if it is high, you might choose to deprioritize services and concentrate on your core business.

- *Inventory turns:* Holding on to excessive or non-productive inventory can be a huge cost to your business. It ties up cash that could be deployed for other purposes. If you can operate well with, say, $100,000 of inventory but have $200,000 worth of the stuff sitting around, that dead inventory takes up more space, depreciates over time and sucks up staff time. It must be faced, dusted, returned when it expires, and counted. And if you choose to hire a third-party inventory company for stock-taking, it will probably charge you based on how much inventory you have. If you can take that extra $100,000 of inventory out of the business and put it into another investment, suddenly it is making money. Or you can take it and buy some automation for your business, reducing the need to pay staff.

- *Basket size/share of wallet:* It is hard to believe that more pharmacies do not measure this, because what could be more valuable to know than how much money you are making on each customer who comes through your doors? It is important to establish your baseline and then find ways to improve it. Maybe you can try additional services and products, or experiment with different merchandising. Or ask yourself: What do your customers walk past on their way to the checkout? Is there a way to entice them to buy one extra thing – and boost your store's basket size? You will not know unless you start measuring it.

- *Wages as a percentage of gross margin:* Most pharmacist-owners will measure their relative wage costs as a percentage of revenue. Yet with the advent of biologics and other very expensive but low-margin medications, that formula can make you look like a hero when you in fact are not. A better metric for measuring your staffing expenses is to divide payroll dollars by gross margin (revenue minus cost of goods sold, or COGS). The result will also be very comparable from pharmacy to pharmacy, since it accounts for the disparity that high – and low-margin products have on revenue.

- *Wage costs per script:* This is an important metric because it can give you an indication of how much your pharmacy is making from dispensing fees and can point to opportunities to improve. Balancing the right blend of pharmacists to technicians is key. Many pharmacy owners have introduced automated processes to lower wage costs per script. Caution is encouraged here, however, as not every pharmacy can realize a ROI on automation.

- *Wait times:* How long is a patient waiting to get a prescription filled? While this remains an important metric, keep in mind that there is good waiting and bad waiting. Good waiting gives your customer more time to go to the front of the store, look around and perhaps purchase something they did not think they wanted before. Bad waiting is when it takes so long to get their meds that they say "to heck with it" and march out of the store to grab a coffee. Another form of bad waiting occurs behind the counter – when one team member is waiting for another team member to finish a task so they can start theirs.

- *Customer surveys:* These can be either formal or informal. Even simply asking a customer or patient "How are we doing?" can reveal valuable insights into ways to improve your operations.

- *Front-of-store and script margins:* Tracking margins in both your prescription and front-of-store is an important activity. One of the key benefits of joining a buying group or a banner program is to add to your buying power and help build store profit margins. Utilizing private-label programs in concert with plan-o-gram implementation and end-cap margin shielding methodologies can invariably build your front-of-store margins.

- *Frequency of dispensing:* In the appropriate circumstances, filling a recurring prescription more often not only might be safer for your customer, but also could provide a boost to your revenue from dispensing fees.

- *Front-of-store contribution:* In today's changing prescription environment, particularly in rural markets, it makes sense to pay attention to your front-of-store business. An average independent in a niche urban setting or rural market should enjoy front store sales volume of $250,000 to $750,000. We've seen some larger-format independent pharmacies with front store volumes exceeding $2,000,000 in annual sales. Ensure, however, that your front-of-store contributes commensurately to its share of wages, rent and other expenses and that it is, in fact, profitable.

Value Driver 2: Growth and scalability

Acquirers typically pay more for businesses with a greater growth rate and/or potential to grow. In rare cases, an acquiring company may even buy a business that scores high on growth potential but low on other attributes, because the acquirer sees a way to leverage some of its own assets to help the business expand much more quickly than it could under its current owner.

Still, many pharmacies will grow in spite of, rather than because of, management. But is the business scalable? A business that is scalable is one in which the owner or manager has done something to cause it to grow. A pharmacy might grow because more people moved into the neighbourhood, but what would make it even more valuable is if the pharmacist-owner has a continuous, repeatable plan to produce growth in the business over the long term. It might mean introducing a new product line or service, making predictions that it will have a certain result, and then measuring that result using a variance report. Such a process reflects a concrete plan that a vendor can show a potential buyer, and it suggests that your pharmacy has value beyond what a suitor can see in front of them.

Value Driver 3: Recurring revenue

Businesses with recurring and predictable revenues are the greatest creator of wealth for astute pharmacy business owners. Such a feature will always attract interested buyers. This is why pharmacy business owners are often able to sell their practices for considerably more money than when a doctor or lawyer attempts to sell their practice. (We refer to such practices as "zero-based" revenue businesses as at the end of every financial year, the lawyer starts from zero!) Buyers are willing to pay more when their perception is that the cash flow of your pharmacy business is substantial, predictable, growing and recurring. That reduces risk in the eyes of the buyer.

Value Driver 4: Concentration risk

Pharmacies that have a concentrated customer and patient base dependent on a physician or two runs the risk of that base leaving to follow a physician elsewhere. A community dependent on one major employer or industry is vulnerable as a result of changing economic circumstances. We refer to such phenomena as concentration risk – the proverbial case of putting all your eggs in one basket. On the other hand, broader community customer bases not dependent on a handful of prescribers or one employer will increase the value of your pharmacy because if one customer leaves, another is there to take their place. And with lower risk comes higher value.

Clinic-based pharmacy practices can be particularly vulnerable to concentration risk. A pharmacy next to a clinic might indeed be earning $100,000 a year in dispensing fees, but if it is completely dependent on that clinic, what happens when the doctors start to retire or are enticed to move to a new medical clinic? A similar situation can occur when pharmacies win limited-term contracts to supply scripts to congregate care homes. It can be a lucrative business, but when the contract runs out the pharmacy has to bid on it again. If its bid loses – and if it has grown overly dependent on that contract over the previous four or five years – then the effect might be devastating.

Because of that concentration risk, and because cash flows can be unpredictable, contract – and clinic-based pharmacy businesses often attract lower prices than others. A pharmacy with similar revenue that is located on Main Street, has plenty of parking, a solid front-of-store operation, and therefore a diversified customer base (and multiple revenue sources) will generally be perceived by buyers as less risky and will command a higher selling price.

Value Driver 5: Reliable financial information

Professionally prepared financial statements are imperative for anyone thinking of selling their pharmacy. Hiring an outside accountant (in addition to a bookkeeper) to prepare your financials is a great investment in the future value of your business. When it comes time to sell, reliable financial records and supporting documentation will assure a potential buyer that your pharmacy is what you say it is. On the other hand, sketchy financial information – with inconsistent or improperly applied accounting practices – will trigger skepticism in a wary buyer. The better the information you can provide, the lower the risk the buyer will apply to the business and the more they will be willing to pay for it. Good, reliable financial statements are a must. Never try to get away with anything less.

Value Driver 6: Taking the "you" out of your business

How well is your store run when you are not there? Do you depend on a single technician or pharmacist to keep things operating smoothly? In other words, how important is the "you" factor to the value of your business? After you sell your pharmacy, chances are that you are no longer going to be standing behind the counter, so if your staff – who presumably will be there – are poorly trained, unmotivated or insufficiently delegated to act responsibly on their own, the value of your business can suffer. Capable, well-trained employees with strong customer relationship skills can make the transfer to a new owner easier, and from a buyer's perspective will increase the chances of patient and customer retention. The lower the transfer risk, the greater the value of the business.

That is why adopting and documenting standard operating procedures (SOPs) can be important in maximizing your pharmacy's value, because they demonstrate that the business can be run profitably after the sale. The goal here is to take the "you" out of your business and show a potential buyer that you do not need to be there to keep it running profitably. Automated procedures can be among your SOPs, and they can add value in a buyer's eyes because they indicate that the business is less reliant on the human element. Another approach is to identify a key staff member (not necessarily a pharmacist, by the way) who has the authority and experience to take charge – even when you are on your shift. If that team member stays on after the sale, then it again lowers transfer risk for the buyer.

Taking the "you" out of your business, however, is something of a balancing act. Sure, we would all like to let our businesses run themselves, collect the profits and go sit on a beach somewhere. Yet pharmacists who try to live this dream might end up facing a big challenge in the form of personal goodwill. If, after years of working hard and building relationships with customers, a pharmacist-owner decides to step back and give more authority (and customer face time) to a delegated staff member, the owner runs the risk of effectively transferring personal goodwill to the delegate. When it comes time for the owner to sell, who does that goodwill belong to? If the owner has abdicated his/her connection to the customer base, the goodwill could belong to the delegate. Therefore, unless the owner has taken steps to ensure that team member will stay on after the sale, transfer risk rises and the value of the pharmacy declines. In fact, we have seen several deals held hostage by key personnel who have not been properly incentivized to stay – and who might be upset that they have not been given a chance to buy the pharmacy themselves. Food for thought!

Value Driver 7: Competitive advantage

Business consultant John Warrillow, author of *Built To Sell*, often talks about "Monopoly of Control" – a concept that answers the question of how well your business is differentiated from your competitors. Essentially, it boils down to how well your business has created its own monopoly. To what degree is it the only place your customers can come for your unique offering of services, products and relationships? Unique, value-added services and products can function as a kind of glue that attaches your customers to your business – hopefully, even after a sale. They create a competitive "moat" that prevents others from copying you and stealing your customers away, and some buyers will pay a premium for businesses that have such barriers.

The advantage can derive from physical attributes of a business, as well – for instance, a good location in a busy part of town or near a clinic, a secure lease, plenty of parking, or an optimal store layout. But what many pharmacists fail to realize is that they can often create their own brand of competitive advantage by concentrating on non-physical aspects of their business, like friendliness of service, efficiency in dispensing, a robust delivery service or community involvement and charity/philanthropic work. If pharmacist-owners can find that secret sauce, they enjoy a competitive advantage over other pharmacies.

Value Driver 8: Customer relationships

How likely are your customers to renew a prescription with you? If they bought something from the front-of-store today, would they buy it there again next time they need it? Do they review your store well on social media? Do they refer friends and family? Trust us: most independent pharmacist-owners are not actively seeking out – or quantifying – the relationship they have with their customers, but corporate competitors do. When assessing the quality of a store's customer relationships, they look for stability, consistency, repeatability, reliability and sustainability as key attributes.

You, as a pharmacist-owner, can take concrete steps to improve on all those counts. A good marketing program can create name recognition (of both the business and its employees), while building customer awareness and loyalty. Operational efficiency and accuracy in prescription output and complimentary professional advice will enhance your pharmacy's reputation in the community, as will well-trained, courteous, customer-centric staff. While the value of your business in part comes from its tangible assets, goodwill comprises most of the price a buyer is willing to pay. "Soft" attributes are builders of goodwill, and therefore of value.

Value Driver 9: Facility decorum and equipment condition

Let us pretend you are in the market for a used car, and you come across two of the same model, year, mileage and basic condition. One of them is spotless inside and out, its body polished to a radiant shine and its interior still redolent of that "new car smell"; the other is caked in road dust, it reeks of stale tobacco inside, and empty fast-food packages litter the floor. Which one would you pay more for? Chances are it would be the first, not only because you would not have to waste your time cleaning it up, but also because its state of cleanliness suggests that the owner has really taken care of it.

The same psychology comes into play when selling your business. Although some buyers will focus almost exclusively on the financial numbers, the physical appearance and condition of your store and equipment can impact the price many buyers are willing to pay. The considerations go beyond the cleanliness of your shelves and floor to include things like the tidiness of your work area and even of your staff. If you give the impression that your store and personnel are messy and careless, a buyer might suspect that your business's operations and documentation are in a similar state of disrepair.

So, if the store is not already neat and tidy, clean it up. Staff should be in uniforms, and their name tags should be prominent, professional and meaningful (that is, they should tell the customer what the team member does). Clutter at the front-of-store will discourage customers from exploring your aisles; get rid of it. Fresh paint is an inexpensive way to create a professional new look, and do not forget to look up to see if the lights and ceiling are clean and free from danglers. These might seem minor considerations, but buyers will take note consciously or subconsciously. Ignore the mess at your own peril.

Value Driver 10: Audit risk reduction

Apologies if we sound like a broken record about risks, but mitigating them remains vital to increasing your pharmacy's value. One of the most important to address is audit risk, and unfortunately it is also one of the most often overlooked. An audit can come in many forms: from narcotic inspectors, third-party payors, tax authorities and, in some jurisdictions, professional service provision monitors. If such risks exist, they will lower the value of your business in the eyes of a buyer. Or worse, they will be averse to an optimum sale structure that could reduce your tax costs at the time of sale. It is important to note that such risks are addressed in the "representations and warranties" section of definitive sale agreements. You can run, but you can't hide!

To avoid audit risk, pharmacist-owners should create or revisit their narcotics-tracking procedures and documentation protocols. They should make sure they adequately document the professional services they provide. Sloppiness and poorly trained staff are the primary factors contributing to third-party payor clawbacks. And finally, they should work with their accountant to assess their business for tax audit risks and liabilities. Doing so will not only help limit the effects of an audit and as a result maintain your pharmacy's value – it is also simply good business.

Value Driver 11: Loss prevention

Losses in a retail pharmacy occur both externally and internally. Many pharmacist-owners fail to take some obvious precautionary steps to prevent revenue from walking out the door. An aware staff trained to make eye contact with all customers can serve as the cornerstone of loss prevention. Up-to-date security equipment and protocols can only go so far towards reducing shrinkage. But an eye towards loss prevention goes beyond ensuring that staff and/or customers are not making off with items for which they have not paid.

Loss prevention also applies to cybersecurity, not just of internal systems but also of IT service providers with whom you might share or store vital patient and business information. It is the pharmacy owner's responsibility to set an example when it comes to loss prevention in the eyes of the store staff.

Value Driver 12: Waste reduction

We are big fans of Lean Six Sigma, a management approach that focuses in part on systematically removing waste from business processes. The system identifies and addresses eight different kinds of waste, and while it can all become quite technical, you do not need to be a Lean Six Sigma Black Belt to become familiar with them and apply them to your own business.

- Defects: Do your prescriptions often get filled in error and require reprocessing?

- Overproduction: How often do you fill prescriptions that no one picks up?

- Waiting: Often overlooked, but when a technician waits for you to complete your task, or you wait for them to complete theirs – that is a waste of resources.

- Non-utilized talent: Your technicians now have an expanded scope of practice, and so do you. Is this being fully utilized?

- Transportation: Is your delivery system as efficient as it could be?

- Inventory: In our experience, most pharmacies have a good handle on their medication inventories; front-of-store, however, often leaves a lot to be desired.

- Motion: Poorly designed dispensaries create a lot of steps. A small capital outlay can make a major difference.

- Extra processing: This is basically all those redundant efforts that serve no purpose. Overly detailed professional services documentation is a common example.

We encourage pharmacy owners to refer to *Pharmacy Management in Canada* (https://www.cfpnet.ca/publications/details/id/3), sponsored by the Canadian Foundation for Pharmacy, for a detailed discussion on drivers of value and effective financial and operational management.

CHAPTER 8:

How To Minimize
Tax Pain

By Mike Stannix CPA, CA, TEP
Partner, Accelerate LLP

From the authors: This in itself might be a cliché, but clichés are clichés for a reason: they tend to be true. And one of the most common – that the only two inevitabilities in life are death and taxes – is also among the most accurate.

We have spoken before about the importance of recognizing one's own mortality when it comes to pharmacy exit planning, but considering the tax implications of selling your pharmacy is arguably just as important. All too often, the frictional tax effects of a sale can be overlooked until it is far too late to minimize them. To effectively do that, pharmacy owners will benefit from the advice of an accountant who has expert knowledge of Canadian tax regulations and experience in interpreting them for the sale of a business.

We are not such individuals, but we know and often work with someone who fits the bill: Mike Stannix. A Chartered Accountant and a Chartered Professional Accountant, Mike has more than a decade of experience in tax compliance, and he has completed CPA Canada's In-Depth Tax Course. (Trust us: it's hard.) Mike has also completed his trust and estate practitioner's (TEP) designation. He has plenty of experience helping small business owners in general and pharmacy owners in particular. So we could think of nobody more qualified to jump in here and provide some useful advice on the tax implications of selling your pharmacy. Over to you, Mr. Stannix...

The worst time to start thinking about the tax ramifications of selling your business is when you get an offer. Unfortunately, in my experience working with business owners, including pharmacy owners, that is usually when they start.

To the uninitiated, the tax rules around selling a business in Canada can seem arcane, complicated and about the furthest thing away from what busy owners want to think about. But they matter. A lot. Depending on the scale of the transaction, an overlooked opportunity to minimize the tax burden of a sale can cost the seller anywhere from hundreds to *hundreds of thousands* of dollars. I have seen it happen. And the sad fact is that these tax costs might well have been avoided if the seller had been armed with a bit of good information and a lot of planning.

That is why, in my view, it is essential for anyone considering selling their pharmacy business to consult with a tax expert before the sale – ideally, years before.

What follows is not intended in any way to take the place of direct expert advice. Every situation is different. The goal here is to introduce some of the general concepts that can affect how taxes come into play in a business sale transaction, to suggest areas to focus on in terms of compliance and tax minimization, and to equip you with some baseline understanding of applicable tax rules so that you can have informed conversations with your accounting team.

Some of you might prefer to watch paint dry than to read about tax rules. I can certainly understand that. But if you are inclined to skip over what follows, then I would urge you to at least take a look at the last section of this chapter, which suggests some important points you should be discussing with your accountant.

If even that is too much for you, please take this key message to heart: when it comes to planning for the tax implications of selling your pharmacy, do not wait until the last minute. A sound tax plan can help you not only save a lot of money, but also help ensure that the biggest liquidity event of your life does not end in regret.

1. Share sale versus asset sale

Anytime someone is looking to sell a business, there are two basic ways to do it. The vendor (seller) can either sell the equity of the company – the shares – or they can sell the assets of the company – the things (not all tangible, by the way) that the business requires to operate, like working capital, equipment, inventory and goodwill. In general, vendors prefer share sales and buyers prefer asset sales, for reasons we will talk about further below.

Advantages of a share sale

Why do vendors generally prefer share sales? One reason is simplicity. In a share sale, the vendor and the buyer do not have to haggle over the value of a whole bunch of different types of assets. That makes the transaction easier to handle for both parties, but professional fees tend to be a little higher than in an asset sale.

Another advantage, from the seller's point of view, is that a share sale helps them close the door, move on and be done with the business. If they are selling equity, then any inherent liabilities of the business are transferred to the purchaser. Of course, transactions often involve legal agreements that could make the seller liable in certain circumstances, but for the most part a share sale offers a clean break. The vendor can walk away and not worry about much afterwards.

Perhaps the biggest advantage of share sales for sellers, however, is the opportunity to claim the lifetime capital gains exemption. When they sell, they will usually realize a (sometimes substantial) capital gain. In Canada, capital gains are currently subject to a 50% inclusion rate (this has not always been the case, and tax legislation can change the inclusion rate), which effectively means the seller will include in their income for tax purposes only half the increase in the value of their business. (We call this the "taxable capital gain.") As well, every Canadian resident is entitled to a one-time lifetime capital gains exemption, which is currently indexed to inflation. This capital gains exemption may be used to offset capital gains. As of the 2021 taxation year, the lifetime exemption stands at around $885,000.

For a very simplistic example, if someone sold their shares in a qualifying pharmacy for a million dollars in 2021 and it cost them only $100,000 to buy the shares 10 years prior, that person would be subject to "normal" tax on only $15,000 ($900,000 being the increase in value minus the capital gains exemption of $885,000) at the time of sale. That is significant tax mitigation.

Why most buyers prefer asset sales

In asset sales, the fundamental assets required to run the business are transferred to the buyer. From the buyer's perspective, this kind of transaction is more efficient, in that they can pick and choose which assets they want to buy and minimize the chances of getting redundant assets they might not need. As well, unlike a share sale, the buyer does not have to worry about whether the company they are buying has any skeletons in the closet, since any liabilities of the selling company are not transferred to the buyer in an asset purchase. It is the mirror image of the liability advantage provided to a seller by a share sale: in an asset sale, the buyer is off the hook.

When it comes to taxes, an asset sale can provide a potential future benefit to the buyer, largely because of the purchase of depreciable assets. Over time, a pharmacy business will depreciate the value of its assets and claim the depreciation as a deduction against income. This results in a "depreciated" asset value. In the case of a share deal, the purchaser buys shares and inherits the low depreciated values of assets already inside the corporation, thus resulting in less depreciation available in the future. However, in an asset deal, the buyer may get a bump in the cost base of the purchased assets and gains the ability to depreciate those assets over time, reaping the correspondent tax advantages. Goodwill, which often counts as a large proportion of assets in the sale of a pharmacy business, is also depreciable for tax purposes, so a purchaser of the business's assets will realize a tax benefit from depreciating goodwill right out of the gate. Meanwhile, on the other side of the table, when a seller sells the assets of the business, the purchase price that is allocated to those assets will be credited against the undepreciated capital cost; if the purchase price exceeds the depreciated value, there could be additional tax to pay.

One potential drawback of an asset transaction for the buyer can come into play if the business's operations rely heavily on financing, which can be difficult to transfer to a new owner since it is tied to the old business. Another challenge can present itself if the corporation has some tax benefits attached to it, such as non-capital losses being carried forward; since the buyer is purchasing assets and not the corporation, those benefits would not be transferred in an asset sale. Still, compared to the advantages of an asset sale, these can be relatively minor considerations for the buyer.

Given all those factors, it is clear why sellers typically prefer share sales and buyers prefer asset sales. However, it is not often a simple matter of the seller choosing one over the other. Rather, the structure of the sale vis-a-vis assets or shares is, in real life, usually a point of negotiation between the buyer and the vendor. Asset type sales outside the pharmacy industry typically command a higher selling price than share sales because the respective parties take into account the different tax and other incentives that each structure offers.

Still, sellers usually favour a share sale. The situation sellers most want to avoid, therefore, is one where they *cannot* complete a share sale – or at least not without paying a huge amount of tax. To avoid that can require a significant commitment in time and planning. If you want to sell your business tax-efficiently through a share sale, it pays to get started early.

2. Preparing for a sale: general concepts

Redundant assets

Several years ago, my firm was involved in a transaction where the person selling his business was quite motivated to make it a share sale. He got his wish, but after the contracts had been signed, the buyers realized that one of the assets of the business they had just purchased was the seller's car – he had neglected to strip it out of the assets of the corporation during negotiations. When the day came for him to turn over the business, the buyers let him know that they were expecting the keys to the automobile too, which came as something of a shock to the seller.

In the end, the buyers gave the car back – at a price – but the seller's misstep provides a good lesson: when you sell your shares of a business, you want to extract any assets you want to keep before you sell it. You also want to carve out any redundant assets (things that the buyer will not use as part of the business – typically real estate or personal assets) from the deal. (Mike and Max on occasion find marketable securities like investment portfolios held inside pharmacy operating companies. Extracting these types of redundant assets invariably will lead to triggering capital gains or losses at the most inopportune time.) Obviously, stripping assets will affect the selling price, but it can also help you avoid some nasty surprises down the road.

There are other specific reasons to extract redundant assets from your business before selling it, as well as various ways to do it tax-efficiently. We will discuss those later in this chapter.

Corporate tax attributes

Understandably, most pharmacists will not pay much attention to the nuances of corporate accounting, but your business may have certain tax attributes that can help you extract capital and minimize the tax implications of selling. These attributes can be very useful when preparing to sell, and prospective sellers should be familiar enough with the concepts to be prepared to discuss them with their tax advisors.

Refundable dividend tax on hand account (RDTOH)

The RDTOH is not a simple thing at all (but at least now you know the abbreviation!). At root, it is a "notional account" that tracks income tax paid by a private corporation at high tax rates on passive investment income. When it distributes dividends, the corporation is also paying out a certain portion of that already-taxed income to shareholders, who then pay the applicable personal tax rate on it again. When that happens, the corporation can receive a dividend refund (or a refund of the high-rate tax paid in the past), which is limited by the balance in the RDTOH account. The business should consider utilizing the balance in the RDTOH account prior to a sale.

General rate income pool (GRIP)

The GRIP balance tracks taxable income from the corporation that has not benefited from the small business deduction or other favourable tax rates. A corporation can declare and pay an eligible dividend up to the balance in the GRIP account. Once an eligible dividend has been paid, the GRIP balance is reduced by the amount of the eligible dividend. The advantage of this account is that eligible dividends are taxed at a much lower tax rate than non-eligible dividends. In Ontario, the top marginal tax rate on eligible dividends is 39.34% in comparison to the

47.74% top marginal tax rate on non-eligible dividends. Accordingly, a shareholder may wish to utilize the balance in the GRIP account prior to a sale. (Check and compare the rates used in the above example in your home province.)

Capital dividend account (CDA)

If a business realizes a capital gain from the sale of an asset, half of the capital gain is included in income for tax purposes (the taxable capital gain) and subject to tax. The other half (the "non-taxable capital gain") is added to the CDA, and the money inside it can be distributed to shareholders as a capital dividend. The huge advantage here is that the cash distributed as a capital dividend is tax-free to the shareholder. So, before a sale, it always advisable to pay out any CDA balance to shareholders and reduce it to zero.

Paid-up capital (PUC)

PUC is the capital you paid into the business for your shares. Before you sell your business, you should be able to have that capital returned to you without having to pay tax on it.

3. Share sales: specific considerations

As we have noted above, share sales typically represent the seller's preferred transaction structure. If you wish to minimize the tax impact (and who doesn't?), then there are a few considerations you should discuss with your accountant well before you plan to sell. Here are some of the most important:

The lifetime capital gains exemption

The big benefit of a share sale for the seller is the ability to claim the lifetime capital gains exemption (LCGE), thanks to which a capital gain of up to approximately $885,000 (as of 2021) may come to you tax-free. The LCGE is also indexed for inflation, and even family members can claim it. Depending on the value of the business and how much the seller is trying to shelter, a good tax plan can take advantage of that family multiplier effect and work to claim the LCGE for the seller's spouse and children in the transaction.

The big catch: QSBC status

So when it comes to selling your business through share sale, the lifetime capital gains exemption can be pretty great, right? But there is a catch, and it's a big one. To claim the LCGE, the shares in your company must meet the Income Tax Act's criteria for being classified as shares of a Qualified Small Business Corporation, or QSBC shares for short. Failing to meet those criteria – or neglecting to do the things you need to do to meet them until it's too late – can create an outsized tax bill at the end of the transaction.

There are three important tests for whether a company's shares qualify as QSBC shares:

- *Two-year holding period*
  The shares you are selling must have been held by you (or a relative) for at least two years before the transaction date. If you bought the business a year ago and tried to sell it through a share sale, the shares would not quality as QSBC shares and the lifetime capital gains exemption would not apply.

- *50% active business asset test*
  This is the one that can really sneak up on people. Two years leading up to a sale, at least half of the company's assets have to be considered active business assets. Receivables, inventory, equipment, business property and goodwill are usually considered active assets. But if, after taking all that into account, excess cash held by the corporation or passive investments (for example, marketable securities, as mentioned earlier) exceeds 50% of the value of the corporation, then you have a problem, because the shares in your pharmacy would not qualify as QSBC shares. So if your pharmacy is worth a million dollars and you have $500,001 in excess cash/passive investments on the books **at any time** during the two years before selling it, then the shares do not quality as QSBC shares and you cannot claim the lifetime capital gains exemption after your sale.
  Let me emphasize that last point because the 50% test is an "at any time" standard. In other words, if active business assets drop below 50% of the company's value *at any time* during the two years before the share sale, it has failed the 50% active business asset test. Theoretically, if you held $500,001 of excess cash/passive investments in your business for one day during the two years before the sale, the shares of your company would not qualify as QSBC shares. No lifetime capital gains exemption.

- *90% active business asset test*
  Once your company has cleared the 50% active asset test, an even higher hurdle awaits. When the sale transaction

closes, 90% of the assets in the business must be active. While this is a stringent test, most business owners who have cleared the 50% hurdle have planned into the 90% threshold, and a good tax advisor (in concert with advisors like Mike and Max) can assist with moving non-active assets out of the business by sale day. (We call this purification: it is one of the key ways advisors can assist a pharmacy vendor during the final weeks prior to the sale date.)

4. Asset sales: specific considerations

While sellers typically prefer share sale transactions for their potential to harness the lifetime capital gains exemption, asset sales can and do occur in the pharmacy industry (in large part because buyers tend to prefer them). They entail several considerations that from a tax perspective are quite different from those for a share sale. Here are the most significant:

Purchase price allocation

Typically, purchase price allocation, or PPA, is a part of the negotiation between the buyer and the seller, and for good reason. Remember: in a typical business, the value of assets depreciates over time and that depreciation is tax deductible. When those assets are sold at a higher price than their depreciated value (as would typically occur in an asset sale), then the seller is realizing "recaptured" value on those assets and is subject to tax on that value. (The purchase price minus the depreciated value, referred to as "recapture.") Accordingly, the seller in an asset sale will be motivated to lower the proceeds on those depreciated assets. On the other side of the table, the buyer may be motivated to go the other way, looking for a higher reset value allocated to those assets with a view to realizing more depreciation going forward. Now, in the real world, these details are typically sorted out by accountants and lawyers, and it is important to recognize that whatever the negotiating goals of each party may be, the allocations must be reasonable – the Canada Revenue Agency will not accept them otherwise.

Restrictive covenants

Often, the buyers of a business want to ensure that the seller will not compete with them directly or go to work for a competitor for a period of time after the transaction. These restrictive covenants attached to the sale of the business should be included in the sale agreement, and any value attributed to them should be clearly stated. Alternatively, both parties can make an election stipulating that no proceeds are attached to the covenants. If the sale agreement does not clearly articulate any value assigned to restrictive covenants, the Canada Revenue Agency could assign what it views to be a reasonable value and then charge you tax on it. Typically, therefore, we usually recommend including an election that no proceeds are attributable to these covenants, just out of an abundance of caution.

HST/GST election (province-dependent)

Selling assets would typically invoke the Harmonized Sales Tax (HST)/ Goods and Services Tax (GST). For efficiency's sake, it's a good idea to make an election in the sale agreement stating that the parties are transferring assets of an entire business and that HST/GST will not be charged. Doing so eliminates a lot of paperwork down the road.

Tax deferral and cash distribution planning

When you sell your pharmacy business's assets, a significant amount of money will (hopefully) be coming into the corporation, which going forward will have no assets – just cash. One way of dealing with all that cash is to do nothing; it just stays in the corporation. Or you can reinvest it and start another business, or put it towards a different kind of asset and earn income. From a tax perspective, this is analogous to kicking the proverbial can down the road, as you will not have to pay personal tax on the original transaction proceeds until you begin to extract them from the company.

At some point, however, you will want to get the cash out of the business, and to do that tax-efficiently will require careful cash distribution planning. What you want to avoid is taking a pile of cash and moving it to yourself, which would invoke a significant personal tax hit. The good news is that the sale of assets and other results of the transaction might kick up your company's CDA and RDTOH balances (see above), and you can potentially use those tax attributes to help move money out of the business in a more tax-efficient way.

5. Tax planning

As we discussed above, the most significant hurdles to completing a share sale are the QSBC share tests. Those require that – at least two years before you plan to sell – the business and its active/inactive asset mix need to get onside of the rules and stay there until the transaction is completed. As importantly, you want to ensure you do that in a way that maximizes potential tax savings.

The following are some of the tools and concepts a good tax advisor may employ to help you do that and position yourself for maximum possible tax savings.

Estate freeze

An estate freeze is one of the most common strategies owners employ leading up to a share sale. Its most significant benefit is that it allows the seller to multiply the lifetime capital gains exemption across several individuals, which helps to maximize tax savings.

Here is how it works: Assume you have a business worth $1 million today, but it is growing and you expect it to be worth $3 million in five years. With an estate freeze, one method is for you to exchange your common shares (sometimes called growth shares) for preferred shares (or fixed value shares) worth $1 million. That allows any new shares in the company to be issued at a nominal amount – say, a dollar or even zero – and those shares can then be issued to a spouse or children, or to an inter-vivos (family) trust with family members as beneficiaries. Essentially, you are freezing the value of your shares and letting all future growth accrue to other family members' shares.

Five years later, you sell your pharmacy for $3 million, as expected. Assuming the issued common shares are held by your spouse and child equally, then you receive a million dollars for your (preferred) shares, and your spouse and child each receive a million for their common shares. Now for the good part: you, your spouse and your child are all eligible for the lifetime capital gains exemption, and each party can claim it against their share of the capital gain.

For illustration purposes, let us consider the tax implications of a hypothetical $3-million capital gain under two scenarios. In the first, the seller owns all the shares in the business and claims their $885,000 lifetime capital gains exemption. In Scenario 2, the estate has undergone a freeze transaction and shares are divided equally among the owner, a spouse and a child. (For simplicity, we will apply 2021 top marginal tax rates applied to capital gains for individual's resident in Ontario and assume no party has any other income.)

Scenario 1:

Capital gain from sale: $3,000,000

LCGE: ($885,000)

Net proceeds taxable as capital gains: $2,115,000

Tax payable: $565,974

Scenario 2:

Capital gain allocated to each shareholder: $1,000,000

LCGE: ($885,000)

Net proceeds taxable as capital gains: $115,000

Tax payable per shareholder: $30,774

Total tax payable (all shareholders): $92,322

AN OUNCE OF PREPARATION

A pharmacist came to us six months before an intended sale. After we looked at the company's financial statements, it was clear that while we could probably help the business meet the 90% active asset test at the time of the sale, there was no way it would pass the two-year 50% active asset test. That left the seller with two alternatives: either sell in six months as intended, but as an asset sale, or wait at least two-and-a-half years while the assets were purified and then conduct a share sale. In this case, the owner was motivated to sell, and with no lifetime capital gains exemption he ended up paying hundreds of thousands dollars more in tax than he would have if his company met the QSBC requirements. A lack of tax planning led to a very hard – and expensive – lesson.

As you can see, the potential tax savings from an estate freeze are substantial. In our example, the strategy resulted in savings of *nearly half a million dollars*.

Timing is everything with an estate freeze. It does not make much sense, for instance, to freeze an estate a year before you plan to sell – most businesses do not typically grow that fast. But if you can confidently project growth over the next five years or so, it can be a very valuable tax strategy.

Purification of company assets

When preparing for a share sale, it is imperative to know whether the shares of your business meet the criteria as qualified small business corporation (QSBC) shares, especially the two-year 50% active asset test. If they do not, then there are a few strategies you can discuss with your advisors to meet the threshold and do it tax-efficiently.

One of the most common is a so-called butterfly transaction. This is a complex strategy, but basically it involves establishing a second corporation with no cross-ownership or shared debt, and then moving non-active assets into it in a tax-efficient manner.

Another method is to use a holding company structure. Non-active assets are moved from the operating company into the holding company. The preferred transaction would then be a sale of the underlying operating company shares, in which case some tax would kick up to the holding company, but most of the value would remain with the shareholders. However, an important proviso applies in situations where an individual holds shares indirectly in the operating company through a holding company. To claim the lifetime capital gains exemption, he or she will have to sell their shares in the holding company, not the operating company, when the business is sold. That can sometimes be challenging because buyers may be hesitant to buy holding company shares. So it is usually advisable to keep the holding company "clean," without cross-ownership of shares or any other transactions not involving the pharmacy running through it.

One important point to remember is that asset purification can be conducted at multiple times during the life of a company, depending on the needs of a company and where the assets need to be. But for the purposes of preparing for a share sale, the process – and starting it in time to ensure your company meets the QSBC threshold – can be especially important.

Income-splitting and TOSI

In 2018, the federal government changed the rules governing tax on split income (TOSI) to be broader in their application, and it had a dramatic impact on small businesses. The changes closed a lot of typical income-splitting strategies for small businesses, such as paying dividends to family members who were not really involved in the business. But the new rules also affected share sales, and that reinforces why it is so important for a company to meet the QSBC test on all accounts.

Remember that the goal in a share sale is for the seller and any shareholding family members to use their lifetime capital gains exemptions, which apply only if the shares of the company are QSBC shares. If QSBC shares are sold, TOSI does not apply; if the shares are divided among family members, each can claim their lifetime capital gains exemption. However, if the shares are non-QSBC shares, not only can shareholders not claim the LCGE, but TOSI also kicks in. Since the owner is effectively splitting income with family members, they will end up paying the highest marginal tax rate on the capital gain. That is yet another reason why it is so important that your company's shares qualify as QSBC shares for the required periods before you sell it.

6. The year-end tax discussion

As Mike and Max have made it abundantly clear in this book, whether you are planning to sell in the immediate future or not, you always want to have an exit strategy. Tax planning should be a big part of that strategy. As a rule of thumb, if you think you even *might* sell in the next five to eight years, then it is time to incorporate that into the year-end discussion with your accountant.

Here are a few things that should be discussed:

- *Identify redundant assets*
  This is an important step towards passing the active asset tests for QSBC status. The idea is to know where your company is in terms of non-active assets and if they are getting close to the 50% threshold (or the 90% threshold if a sale is imminent). If they are, do you need to conduct an asset purification? Or perhaps use a different corporate structure to move those assets out of the company? Now is a good time to have those conversations with your accountant.

- *Get externally prepared financial statements*
  The key question is, Do you have any? The pharmacy industry is (in my experience) notorious for not having recent, externally prepared financial statements at the ready. (Some have *never* had them.) Many simply use internally prepared statements for their tax filings. But when they go to sell their business, externally prepared statements are the first things a potential buyer will want to see.

If you do not have them, then you will be scrambling right out of the gate. It is far better to just get it done every year.

- *Check corporate tax attributes*
  Identify what the balances are in your RDTOH, GRIP, CDA and PUC accounts, and discuss whether, when and how you might want to get those balances to zero.

- *Assess your estate planning needs*
  Timing is everything. Discuss what the value of your company is today. If you are the only shareholder and you think the business is worth more than the lifetime capital gains exemption, then it might be the right time to implement an estate freeze. If the business is worth a *lot* more than the LCGE and likely will not grow much in future, you may have missed the boat. The annual accountant meeting is also a good time to assess whether a holding company structure might be appropriate for your business.

- *Consider the effect of Subsection 55(2) of the Income Tax Act on intercorporate dividends*
  It used to be relatively easy for owners of multiple businesses to move cash from one company to another without a tax hit, thanks to an exemption for intercorporate dividends. However, the government recently expanded the rules under Subsection 55(2) of the Income Tax Act to prevent surplus stripping. Don't worry if you don't know what that means – the effect is that cash paid as a dividend to another corporation (typically received tax-free) to reduce a future capital gain could be taxed as a capital gain to the recipient corporation. Business owners just have to be careful, and owners of multiple companies should at

least have the discussion with their accountant to make sure that Subsection 55(2) does not apply to intercorporate dividends.

- *Consider other tax planning strategies*
  In this chapter, I have mentioned a few commonly used tax planning strategies, but there are many more. Speak to a trusted tax advisor about whether another strategy may be more suited to your needs and plans.

- *Prepare a strategic wealth plan*
  It is vital that you be confident that when you eventually do sell your pharmacy business, you will have sufficient financial assets to retire on and continue to sell at the level of comfort you have come to expect. (This is a very important topic that is discussed in further detail in the next chapter.)

You should be able to tell by now that preparing for the sale of your business well in advance can pay huge dividends. In all too many cases, however, pharmacists do not begin to think about taxes until they have an offer on the table. By then, it is often too late to transact the sale in the most tax-efficient way. Failing to meet the QSBC standard is a common lapse, and it usually occurs for one reason: the pharmacist-owner never talked about it with their accountant.

You now know the basics of the tax implications of selling your pharmacy. If you are thinking about selling somewhere down the road, then it is probably time for you to begin to have serious conversations with your accountant about the tax consequences and how you will implement strategies to realize the biggest tax benefits. I encourage you to do so in concert with an experienced financial advisor familiar with the nuances of being a small business owner. (Particular knowledge in pharmacy is a bonus.) Retaining a qualified transaction advisor will remove the knowledge burden from you and help ensure a more tax-efficient and profitable sale. In short, you don't need to be a tax expert – you just need to know which questions to ask. Hopefully, at this point, you now have a good idea of what those are.

CHAPTER 9:

Legal Implications

We are not lawyers, nor do we profess to be legal experts in any way, shape or form. That said, we have been involved in enough business transactions to know that the legal issues around selling a pharmacy – which are very often rooted in events that occurred before the selling process – can present significant hurdles to a smooth sale and a satisfactory (and lucrative) outcome.

This can happen in a few ways. Unresolved legal concerns can undermine the willingness of a potential buyer to close a deal, and even if they are willing to buy, legacy legal exposures might well lower the price they are willing to pay. In some circumstances, legal agreements that you have lived with for years while you were operating your pharmacy can end up restricting you when you decide to sell it, preventing you from reaching the broadest possible universe of potential buyers, which again can lower the ultimate price. And finally, in extreme circumstances, legal issues can prevent a sale altogether, leaving you literally holding the bag – with a company you had hoped to exit.

Given the importance of legal considerations when selling your business, it is absolutely imperative that any pharmacist-owner retain a qualified, experienced lawyer as part of their transition team. In addition, as with other aspects of selling a business, it behooves a potential seller to begin considering and resolving legal issues well before the planned sale.

It goes back to a recurring theme in this book: as much as possible, plan the ending from the beginning. Too many times, we have seen pharmacist-owners come to the table not-so-blissfully unaware that the legal agreements they signed in the past could adversely impact the sale of the business. So, even if you do not plan to sell your pharmacy for many years down the road, it makes sense before signing any contract that may impact your eventual exit to discuss it with your lawyer.

In this chapter, we will discuss some of the more important legal considerations for pharmacy owners, with some specific notes on how they might affect the value of your pharmacy and the sale outcome. We will briefly look at governing statutes and regulations, explore the fundamentals of contracts, and then review some of the more common types of contracts and what pharmacist-owners should watch out for. The point is not to train you as a legal expert – we would not be qualified to do that anyway. Rather, we simply want to make you aware of the important contractual and other legal issues we have encountered in our decades of helping pharmacist-owners. With this awareness, you will be better able to recognize the risks and ask your legal counsel the right questions.

With sound advice and a little bit of foreknowledge, the good news is that none of these potential challenges is insurmountable.

1. Statutes, regulations and governing bodies

A straightforward way to think about your pharmacy business as a legal entity is to consider that it operates under various legal frameworks. One is the government framework, which sets out the rules and regulations to which every pharmacy must adhere. In Canada, pharmacy falls under provincial jurisdiction, and the statutes and regulations can differ. As well, Canada has adopted the self-regulatory model for pharmacy, which means that each province has its own pharmacy governing body – the Ontario College of Pharmacists, the B.C. College of Pharmacy, the Newfoundland & Labrador Pharmacy Board, and so on – that has the authority to govern community pharmacies and implement the regulations. The result of these statutory and regulatory frameworks is that the rules for operating and owning a pharmacy vary from province to province.

In practice, many of the interprovincial differences have to do with allowed scope. For instance, at the time of writing this, a pharmacist in Ontario can prescribe for an interim supply, while a pharmacist in Manitoba cannot; pharmacists in Alberta can order lab tests, but they are not allowed to do so in British Columbia. Yet with regard to selling your pharmacy, the pertinent regulations apply to corporate structure, and they, too, can vary from province to province, although there are some similarities. For example, in most jurisdictions, a majority of directors on a pharmacy's board must be licensed pharmacists. Some jurisdictions go further, and place restrictions on *ownership* structure. For example, in Ontario, pharmacists or pharmacist professional corporations must collectively own a majority of the issued shares of each class of a corporation.

Obviously, such restrictions limit the number of potential buyers for a pharmacy in these jurisdictions, and the ramifications of a sale on ownership structure must be taken into account during the selling process. As well, ownership requirements can present challenges to efficient tax planning, especially involving holding corporations, estates and inter-vivos (family) trusts. So it is advisable to discuss these potential issues with your legal counsel and your tax accountant.

2. Contracts

Beyond the statutory and regulatory frameworks, pharmacies also operate (like other businesses) within the parameters of the common law. This is the realm of contracts, which function in the pharmacy ecosystem in several areas. In general, contracts define a pharmacy's significant commercial relationships – with banks, with landlords, with banner provider groups, with wholesalers, and so on.

Through the life cycle of your business, you will, of course, sign a lot of contracts, and many if not most of them will be presented to you as "standard agreements." These have their uses because they normalize a whole bunch of terms and conditions that often are seen not to require much negotiation. In short, they are efficient and practical. But "efficient and practical" for whom? Just because a form is "standard" does not mean it is fair. Standard agreements are often presented by one party and the other party is given little or no room to negotiate – a "take it or leave it" proposition. The fact remains, however, that no legal contract exists until both parties sign it.

Because of that, you usually can and often *should* try to actively negotiate any contract before you sign it. There are some exceptions; contracts with third-party non-government payors like insurance companies and with government health programs really are take-it-or-leave-it propositions. Still, we have always been reluctant to recommend a pharmacist just accept an agreement because it is "standard." Mortgage agreements, leases, wholesale and banner agreements – there might be standard forms for all of these, but you can also negotiate in each of these cases to arrive at a contract that is fairer to you.

At the very least, starting from the position that you are going to negotiate every contract will force you to actually read the thing. In our experience, many pharmacist-owners don't do this; in fact, we would hazard a guess that a large majority of pharmacist-owners have signed a contract without thoroughly understanding it or getting a third-party opinion from a lawyer first, and then they suffer the consequences down the road.

Our advice: Do not sign anything until you know what you are signing. There are a number of terms and conditions in a typical contract that you need be aware of: the who, the what, the how much, and the how long, along with each party's respective rights and obligations. It is also vital, though often overlooked, to pay attention to collateral issues – for instance, the question of what kinds of security you provide to suppliers.

Remember that having strong, fair contracts for your business will ultimately preserve and perhaps even increase the value of your business. An informed buyer – and you must always assume that they *are* informed – will look carefully at the quality of your pharmacy's contracts when deciding whether to buy and how much to offer.

So pay close attention to your company's contracts. As a rule, if you do not understand them, do not sign them. And if you have any concerns about how the contracts you have already signed might impact the eventual sale of your business, talk to your lawyer, as you may have an opportunity to negotiate changes before you start the sale process.

3. Wholesale supply agreements

Although there are technically many companies in Canada that supply molecules to retail pharmacies, it would be generous to say that the wholesale pharmaceutical supply industry is an oligopoly. There is, in fact, only one major national wholesaler at the time of this writing, and just a handful of relevant regional wholesalers. This concentration of market power has, in our view, some potential for anti-competitive behaviour and predatory pricing, yet the reality is that retail pharmacy occupies such a small corner of the Canadian business environment that policymakers are realistically less interested as a matter of public health policy. While having control of the distribution of the country's pharmaceutical supply in the hands of a few entities might (or should) raise a public policy concern, we doubt that this "oligopolistic" environment will change anytime soon.

Anyway, that is probably a battle for another day.

In the real world, most pharmacist-owners encounter wholesale supply agreements by way of a "standard form," facilitated by the banner organization. These agreements can provide a number of benefits to the pharmacist-owner, including beneficial pricing, discounts for prompt payment and other incentives. Realizing these benefits generally requires the pharmacist-owner to follow the rules of the primary agreement, although some do not. The supply agreements also typically stipulate arrangements for occasions when a primary molecule is not available and latitude to substitute secondary molecules in such cases.

Again, these wholesale supply agreements are usually presented to the pharmacist-owner as a standard form contract, but the reality is that you *can* negotiate some aspects of the relationship – we know because we have negotiated them on behalf of our clients. If you cannot negotiate with the banner, then perhaps you are dealing with the wrong banner, and an experienced advisor knows where the boundaries are and the areas of potential movement, based on their experience. The fact is, however, that the current wholesale environment means that the boundaries have become less flexible and more restrictive.

Still, even if there is little room to negotiate, owners should read the contract and sign it only when they thoroughly understand it. The most important consideration with any contract, including a wholesale supply agreement, is to know what your rights, benefits and obligations are, and pay particular attention to issues such as product and return policies, termination provisions, hold-over provisions and of course the term of the contract itself.

One "watch-out" in these agreements is the type of security they demand for payment. In the past, wholesalers would typically claim a purchase money security interest, or PMSI, which in the event of non-payment would allow them to simply repossess the supplies. More recently, however, suppliers are often demanding a much broader security interest, in the form of a general security agreement, or GSA. We are now seeing more wholesale agreements that include not only liability for the corporation, but also personal liability. Those can become important when you are in the process of selling your business, so talk to your lawyer and understand the implications of providing a GSA well beforehand.

4. Third-party payor agreements

As mentioned earlier, these leave little or no room for negotiation. When you are dealing with big insurers like Blue Cross and Green Shield, or government programs like the Ontario Drug Benefit and

Alberta Blue Cross, a pharmacy typically signs a standard form agreement and accepts its terms – namely, the ability to bill the government or third-party insurers, who are good for the money, resulting in higher-quality accounts receivable for the business. There are some potential pitfalls, including the risk of audit experiences resulting in revenue recaptures that can seem pretty draconian and potentially mean-spirited (and which give you limited rights to appeal). In general, though, such dangers do not amount to a reason not to sign a third-party payor agreement. Just don't consider that statement as permission to not even read it!

5. Banner Agreements

The banner agreement is probably the most important contract any pharmacist-owner will sign. Signing on with a buying group such as PharmaChoice, Pharmasave or McKesson's retail banner group (Guardian and IDA, Remedy's RX) does provide some pretty clear benefits: branding, buying power, marketing support (promotions, flyers, etc.), private-label access and loyalty programs, to name a few. Sometimes, pharmacist-owners can access resources like store planning, if they are looking to renovate, as well as operational support. Banner-provided dispensary software and point-of-sale systems are also in the mix, and banners can sometimes help negotiate tech contracts and support.

There is, however, a price to be paid for all those benefits. Under banner agreements, costs can run high, and many have an auto-renewal, or "evergreen," clause that sees the contract renewed automatically six months before the current contract expiry. And to varying degrees, banner agreements can restrict a pharmacist-owner's autonomy – including when it comes time to sell. For instance, many agreements include a right of first refusal (or ROFR) in favour of the banner, which can limit the field of potential buyers for your business.

ROFRs came into common practice as a way to afford some legitimate protections for banner operators, who did not want to see pharmacist-owners just "take the money and run" and have the store leave the banner. Yet we have witnessed ROFRs evolve over time to the point where it can be argued that they can create several potential impediments to the free trade of your business to a buyer. For one thing, they could limit to whom you can sell, and that can adversely impact the realized value of your pharmacy business. In the worst-case scenario, a ROFR could mean that the buyer you must deal with is not the one to whom you would prefer to sell, if the banner has a candidate it would prefer to own and operate the store.

Another potential pitfall of banner agreements: some include claw-back or repayment clauses that kick in when you sell your pharmacy. In such cases, if the pharmacist-owner received any pre-payments or professional allowances for services not yet satisfied under the terms of the agreement, the banner could claw a portion if not all of the advances back.

As well, some ROFRs are so complicated that compliance with the terms is a challenge and can potentially delay or derail attempts by the owner to complete a sale.

Given these risks, the rule for banner agreements is the same as for any contract. Retain expert advice about the negotiable elements of the contract, consult your legal counsel, and know what you are signing.

6. Commercial Leases

After the cost of goods sold and payroll, occupancy expenses (i.e. rent) can be one of the more expensive line items in your company's profit-and-loss statement. Obviously, the amount you pay your landlord should be market-competitive, but there is more to a solid lease than price – and it is important that you do not simply agree to whatever lease agreement the landlord puts in front of you. We always recommend that pharmacist-owners retain a lawyer to help negotiate and properly document their leases. We have seen so many cases where clients come to us to sell their business or valuate it, and we find something in the lease that depresses its value or restricts the ability to sell readily.

So what should you pay attention to? One aspect of a good lease is an exclusive-use clause, which is a form of restrictive covenant that ensures a competitor does not open next door. So if your pharmacy is located in a plaza, for instance, the clause guarantees your business is the only pharmacy operation in it.

Also, pay close attention to terms and renewal clauses. We like to recommend that a lease's unexpired term should be equivalent to a typical mortgage amortization period – say around 10 or 12 years. Why? Think of it from the buyer's perspective: if the business they want to acquire does not have a long-term commercial lease, banks will be hesitant to finance the purchase. In reality, most leases have five-year terms, but pharmacist-owners can negotiate extensions; for instance, a five-year term followed by a five-year option at an agreed rate, followed by two-by-five-year terms that are optional for the business owner at future dates. There is something to be said for ensuring certainty in your business!

Now, you might be surprised how quickly five or 10 years goes by, so when you sign a lease, diarize those end dates. In order to keep an unexpired term of satisfactory length, when a renewal is exercised, consider negotiating a further right to renew so there is always sufficient term to satisfy a potential purchaser. We have even seen some pharmacy operators "surprised" by a lease expiring and finding the lease being scooped up by a competitor! When a lease ends, it typically reverts to a month-to-month arrangement, which has some obvious advantages and disadvantages from an operational standpoint. But from the perspective of someone wanting to sell their pharmacy, it is not a good scenario: if your lease is month-to-month, vendors will find it difficult to find a buyer for their business.

Leases typically include many other terms that may affect the value of your pharmacy. Sometimes, they feature signage rights and restrictions, built-in parking charges and security for payment that could invoke personal, in addition to corporate, liability. All of these can impair the price a buyer is willing to pay. As well, it makes sense to negotiate a lease agreement with assignment privileges, meaning that the next owner can simply take over the lease when you sell. Such agreements often come with clauses that stipulate you must notify the landlord in the event of a transfer of ownership, which is reasonable – but you do need to be aware of your obligations. That being said, the starting point for most sophisticated landlords is a lease that requires the prior consent of the landlord to be obtained in order to assign a lease or to complete a change of control of a corporate owner.

The bottom line: read your lease thoroughly and retain a lawyer who is familiar with its terms.

A last word...

We will end this chapter the way we began it: by urging you to retain an experienced, qualified lawyer to help you negotiate contracts and understand your rights and obligations before you sign. And we reiterate what we said several chapters ago, that not all lawyers are created equal. There are estate, tax and corporate lawyers, and while some can perform the functions of all three satisfactorily, retaining legal counsel with corporate experience in the pharmacy industry would be ideal. Whichever legal counsel you retain as part of your transition team, your team Quarterback should be empowered to reach out to other lawyers as their expertise is needed – and your chosen lawyer should be ready and willing to play nicely in the sandbox.

The legal implications of selling your business are serious stuff, and they often begin long before you begin the process of selling. The best way to understand and address those issues is through foresight, collaboration and shared expertise – a paradigm that will save everybody, but most importantly you, a lot of time and effort and will maximize the return on your investment.

CHAPTER 10:

Strategic Wealth Planning

We have emphasized throughout this book the importance of adopting the right mindset about your pharmacy. It is understandable that when you are starting up and growing your business, you might be so wrapped up in day-to-day operational and financial issues that it is hard to see the big picture – that your pharmacy is an investment, and ideally, one that will help sustain you and your family after your professional life as a pharmacist comes to an end.

When looked at through the investment lens, the sale of your business – although a significant liquidity event, or at least one hopes so – is not the end of the story. Instead, it is simply a new and very different chapter in the "narrative" of your family's wealth. And that chapter, at least in the broad outlines, should be written long before you sell your pharmacy.

That task does not need to be seen as an exercise in fortune-telling. What we mean by writing your retirement narrative is simply this: develop a robust and goals-based strategic wealth plan, ideally with the support of a competent and committed financial advisor.

Thousands, perhaps millions, of volumes have been written on the art and science of wealth planning, and our goal here is not to provide a comprehensive discussion of its practices and principles. Instead, we want to focus on what we have found to work best for our clients, and to highlight a few guidelines and issues that are important for a pharmacist-owner to consider with respect to selling their business. Every owner has different circumstances, needs and goals, so please consider what follows as food for thought – and fodder for discussion with your own financial advisor.

The strategic wealth plan is not just a vital – and sometimes overlooked – *part* of your overall exit planning, but also *informs* the exit process itself. Many pharmacists begin the process of exiting their business by asking themselves, "When do I want to sell?" But before they can really answer, they need to contemplate a whole bunch of other questions: "When do I want to retire?" "What do I want to do in retirement?" "How much money do I need to maintain my desired lifestyle in retirement?" "How will I manage, grow and draw down on my nest egg in retirement?" "How and how much do I want to leave to my family or to philanthropic causes?"

A robust strategic wealth plan can help you answer those and other questions. So it is crucial to get started early and to ensure that the sale of your business is integrated into your long-term financial plan. In other words, the time to start thinking about how you are going to manage your retirement and the proceeds from selling your business is *not* the day after you sell your business.

"Start early" is an important theme in this book, and we do not wish to beat it to death. But let us just point out that the reasons are many for preparing a strategic wealth plan long before you sell your pharmacy business. For one thing, the foundations of a sound retirement plan typically need to be built over time, and steps you take in advance of selling your business can help ensure an efficient allocation, use and eventual transfer of wealth after retirement. For another, as we have pointed out earlier, the transition from pharmacist-owner to retiree is often a difficult one from a psychological perspective; knowing that the sale of the business is part of a long-term plan can go a long way towards reducing stress and increasing peace of mind. And finally, a strategic wealth plan can help set your goals and parameters when it comes time to sell your pharmacy business – and can even help you decide when that time should be.

Before we delve further, we'd like to distinguish between a financial plan and a *strategic* wealth plan. A strategic wealth plan incorporates *all* the financial assets held by a family with the after-tax value estimates of a family business as well as real assets like income property, as an example. Many financial planners tend to focus on the certainty of financial assets with their modelling, and they often ignore other important and material assets and the modelling required to estimate the frictional costs associated with tax. So, if you have not begun working with a competent, experienced financial advisor to develop a strategic wealth plan, you had better get started.

1. The pharmacy wealth journey

Earlier in this book, we outlined the value-based life cycle of a pharmacy business (see Chapter 4). When we look at the business from the perspective of strategic wealth planning, we can apply a similar lens and see how your wealth creation and management journey develops along a continuum. Each phase presents different needs and emphasis when it comes to financial planning.

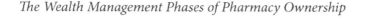

The Wealth Management Phases of Pharmacy Ownership

Let's look at each of these phases in a little more depth:

Wealth creation

In the early stages of their ownership career, pharmacist-owners need to focus on running an efficient business that meets the needs of their patients and customers in the community they serve. The goal here is to improve the profitability of the business and therefore, ultimately, its value. While those just starting out are often most concerned with paying off their business mortgage loans, a host of day-to-day and longer-term issues can come into play, from deciding on the best banner and wholesale alternatives to partnering with other pharmacists to purchase more stores and expand the revenue base. Yet throughout, managing and improving operational efficiency to maximize cash flow not only fortifies the owner's ability to service their debts, but also maximizes the intrinsic value of the business. As the business matures and grows, tax planning and corporate structure re-engineering become important considerations.

Mature Owner/Operator

In this phase, the pharmacist-owner has established their business and is earning surpluses. Concerns about paying off debt no longer apply. Typically, this phase begins when the owners hit their 50s or 60s, they are no longer as interested in expanding, and they are wondering how much longer they wish to operate at their current pace. They might have children who are thinking of joining the family business or junior partners looking to acquire an ownership stake. Ideally, owners have by this point organized their business so that they have surplus cash residing within tax-efficient corporate structures; managing and protecting those surpluses appropriately becomes a focus. They are beginning to contemplate slowing down or retiring.

Transition into Retirement (Post-sale)

Everyone would like to think that after the sale of a profitable business, the former owner will be left with a generous enough nest egg to let them sail off into the figurative sunset of a happy, comfortable and prosperous retirement. Hopefully, if you follow the guidelines we have presented here, the liquidity event that is the sale of your pharmacy will indeed provide a sizable return on your many years of hard work. Yet even if that turns out to be the case, in many ways the post-sale period can be when the hard part really begins.

As a business owner, you have probably enjoyed years of recurring cash flow – profitable pharmacies are really good at that! But once you sell the business, a large portion of your wealth will be tied up in a world of volatile and uncertain capital markets that tend to provide aperiodic returns. From a wealth management perspective, what is important to you quickly changes. Your focus will shift from building and operating your business to protecting your newfound capital.

For entrepreneurs, this can be a strange and challenging landscape. Suddenly, you are subject to the vicissitudes of the economy and of the financial markets, and the long-term low-interest rate environment can be a headwind to the rate of return from your nest egg. To achieve your lifestyle dreams, it is important to re-calibrate your expectations and your priorities. As an entrepreneur, your wealth is created by "concentrating risk"; as an investor, your wealth is preserved by "diversifying risk." Note the difference in mindset.

This is where strategic wealth planning begins to pay dividends, because if you have a plan, you already have figured out your goals and objectives and how you are going to realize them once your business has been sold. The plan will guide you and your family through a maze of issues, and it will provide a road map to proper asset allocation to protect your capital and earn a return on the fruits of your work.

The plan will also identify the amount of risk measured by volatility that your investment advisor will be required to expose your finances to, in order to achieve the goals and objectives identified during the strategic wealth planning process.

2. The strategic wealth planning process

We just referred to a wealth plan as a road map, but it should not be written in stone. Like real-life road systems, the realities of your financial situation will probably change over time, as new avenues of opportunity, alternate routes to your goals and sudden, hopefully temporary roadblocks present themselves. That is why it is important to think of a strategic wealth plan not just as a report, but as a process – something that will adapt to your circumstances as they evolve.

Furthermore, a strategic wealth plan should not be "loaded" with the end result of your financial advisor selling you a product. For instance, the insurance industry can often try to scare their prospects into buying insurance to mitigate some theoretical risk identified in a financial plan.

When we consider wealth planning as a process, it might look something like this:

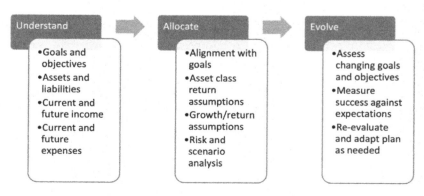

Understand

Of course, if you don't know where you're going, you are highly unlikely to ever get there. So defining your goals is the first and most crucial step in the wealth planning journey. Do you dream of a winter home in the sun? Do you want to golf every day of the year? Do you wish to leave a substantive legacy to your children?

All of these are positive goals, but there are some less salubrious ones that you should also consider. For instance, many retirement plans fail to consider the costs of long-term care or home care for the retiree's later years (and those of their loved ones). You might not want to think about a time when you will depend upon healthcare professionals to support you, but those days are in all probability coming. And it would likely be unwise to count on the government to pay for the level of care you need or desire. Everyone wants a retirement that is "free from care," but we strongly encourage our clients to incorporate the likely expenses of long-term care into their strategic wealth plans.

Beyond defining where you want to go in retirement (your goals), another initial step in the wealth planning process is to assess and fully understand your starting point – how much you have now, how much you are earning and are likely to earn, and how much you are spending now and are likely to spend in future. So this exercise in stock-taking involves detailing your corporate and personal assets and liabilities, your current income and future expected income, and your current expenses and future expected expenses. The process of understanding also requires a clear-eyed analysis of current financial risks and vulnerabilities.

Allocate

This is where the rubber hits the road, but how you invest the money you have put away for retirement is simply a function of the goals, objectives and time horizons identified during your strategic wealth planning process. That sounds easier than it might be in real life, however. Perhaps it is human nature, but we have found that people with a substantial pool of capital often believe their top priority should be to turn it into a much larger pool of capital. Growing wealth is always welcome, of course, but it can come at a cost because risk and return are positively correlated. The higher the return you wish to achieve, the higher the risk you will usually have to assume. Wealth protection and preservation become higher priorities in your investment management than when you were earning a healthy and predictable income as a pharmacist-owner.

This is not to say that risk is "bad" or that a retirement portfolio needs to be or should be zero-risk. It is just to emphasize that risk (and therefore expected return) must be aligned with your individual goals as clearly defined in your strategic wealth plan. In practice, that plan provides you with the discipline to make appropriate decisions when allocating your investments, armed with a clear understanding of risk exposure. And because it is goals-based, the wealth plan identifies the expected rate of return you need to earn on your investments to achieve the lifestyle you envision in retirement. With that knowledge, a good financial advisor can present you with various scenarios for retirement – including some perspective on when and how you should exit your business.

Evolve

Planning for retirement is a journey, but so is retirement itself. The needs and goals of you and your family can and probably will change, so your wealth plan needs to remain flexible along with them. We recommend regular re-assessments of your finances and objectives, as well as measuring the success of your investments against your expectations. Over time, other elements of the financial plan might need to be adapted, especially as family succession and estate issues become more pressing concerns.

Note: A bonus arising from developing a strategic wealth plan is that the resultant net worth statement embedded in a strategic wealth plan can greatly assist an estate lawyer in creating or updating your will.

3. Strategic wealth planning in the context of your business exit

We have discussed how a sound strategic wealth plan provides a guide for investment decisions based on your financial circumstances, needs and goals. It answers the question, "What mix of asset classes should I invest in to meet my objectives?" But the plan also can answer two of the most common questions we hear from pharmacist-owners: "Do I have enough money to retire?" and "When should I sell my business?"

From the point of view of wealth planning, these are really just one question because they both are asking about the optimal time for a business exit. Your strategic wealth plan can help you triangulate the answer. With an understanding of goals and objectives and of the current and future value of the pharmacist-owner's assets (including, of course, the pharmacy), income and expenses, a competent financial advisor can provide plenty of insight into whether you should sell the business now, sell it at a later date, or maintain ownership in your retirement, perhaps hiring a business manager to oversee operations. (We also note that several other factors, like personal health and the status of the retail pharmacy world, must be taken into consideration.)

Let us look at two real-life examples (courtesy of Jason Heath, a Certified Financial Planner with whom we often collaborate) to illustrate how this works. The benchmark against which the following scenarios are measured is the pharmacist-owner's net worth at age 90 (a reasonable estimate of life expectancy these days).

- Mary and John (not their real names) are both 53 years old, and both are pharmacists. They plan to retire in 10 years but lately have begun to wonder if they might be able to afford to do so earlier. So let's do the math, beginning with their current assets and expenses. They have $3.1 million in investments, their pharmacy has been valued at $1.4 million, and their current lifestyle expenses total $137,000 annually. Their pharmacy is a good business but has little growth potential, so we will assume a 1% valuation growth over the next five years and 0% thereafter. If they stick to their current plan and sell the pharmacy in 10 years, then invest the proceeds at a relatively modest 5.25% annual return, their net worth at age 90 will be about $7 million. However, if Mary and John were to sell in five years rather than 10 and invest the proceeds at the same conservative rate of return, their expected net worth in 37 years would be about $8 million. Taking into account their expected post-retirement income and expenses, this comparison suggests not only that Mary and John can afford to retire earlier than planned, but that they quite possibly should.

- Another pharmacist couple – let's call them Maria and Jim – are both 50 years old. Their pharmacy business is highly profitable and has strong growth potential, but they would like to retire as soon as possible. They have $8.5 million in investments, their pharmacy is valued at $6.8 million, and their annual expenses total $150,000. If we run various scenarios based on the same expected rate of return on investment as for Mary and John, Maria and Jim would have a net worth of about $71 million at age 90 if they sold the pharmacy next year. If, however, they waited five years before exiting, their net worth would be $82 million at age 90. And finally, if they never sell their business and instead hire a manager at a salary of $120,000 a year, their net worth at 90 would be a whopping $121 million.

These examples are presented here only for illustrative purposes. Everyone is different, as are their goals and aspirations for retirement, and net worth at age 90 will not be the right metric to apply in every case. (Furthermore, many pharmacy owners may not be as well-heeled as those in the two scenarios depicted above.) There are usually other considerations from a risk and lifestyle perspective. For Maria and Jim, continuing to own their pharmacy might be the logical thing to do on paper, but doing so would also mean that a large proportion of their wealth will be in one asset for a very long time – a clear concentration risk. As well, the prospect of never really "retiring," and of being tied to their business for the rest of their lives, might not be particularly appealing to them.

That is why strategic wealth planning is not just an exercise in running the numbers. It is – or should be – a very personal process that begins and ends with you and your family's goals and aspirations:

what they are, how you plan to achieve them, and how you will tell whether you did.

4. Wealth transfer: Trusts and Gifting

Planning the sale of your pharmacy business is a big undertaking, and your business exit should be integrated into your strategic wealth plan. Selling your business will also have a significant impact on your plans for wealth transfer, making estate planning an important consideration. The fundamental question such planning answers is this: How will you ensure that the wealth you have amassed over your career will be distributed efficiently and effectively to your loved ones or other recipients before, during, and after your retirement?

Obviously, a will that reflects your wishes and your assets is imperative. But while you are alive, there are strategies for wealth transfer that may help maximize both the current and the future value of the proceeds from the sale of your pharmacy business.

Discretionary family trusts

A trust is a legal relationship between three separate parties in respect of specific property: the settlor, who sets up the trust, contributes assets and instructs how they will be managed, and decides who receives benefits from the trust; the trustee, who is appointed by the settlor to control and manage the assets in the trust (the settlor may also be the trustee); and the beneficiaries, who will benefit from the assets owned by the trust.

We will concentrate on *inter-vivos* trusts, often referred to as "trusts of the living." These are established for the purpose of transferring the benefit from owning assets (your business, stocks, cash, etc.)

to certain individuals like your children, without giving up control of the assets to the beneficiaries. The Income Tax Act treats a trust as a separate legal entity for tax purposes. If properly structured, trust income can be allocated to your beneficiaries and taxed in their hands, which can be beneficial if your children pay tax at a lower marginal rate on income earned on the asset than you would.

In many cases, a discretionary family trust will allow pharmacy owners to maintain control of the ownership while permitting certain future benefits to be transferred to other family members. Among those benefits is multiple use of the lifetime capital gain exemption, as our friend Mike Stannix discussed in the chapter on tax implications. As well, shareholders who own more than 10% of their company and do not need all the cash flow from their company can utilize a trust to maintain a tax deferral advantage provided by their company, while transferring investment assets from the active business company to maintain qualification for the capital gain exemption. Typically, a separate investment corporation is created and named as a beneficiary to the family trust, and dividends received by the family trust can be allocated to the investment corporation. These dividends flow from the family trust to the investment corporation tax-free, as they are considered inter-corporate, which can provide a tax deferral benefit. As a result, a larger pool of funds remains available for investment than if the amounts were paid to the shareholder as a salary or bonus. Depending on the province, the tax deferral benefits can be quite substantial, and since the transferred capital is invested, those benefits can grow quickly.

Discretionary trusts also have other potential benefits. One is asset protection. A trust can provide some protection against exposure of its assets to creditors; because all distributions are at the discretion of the trustees, the beneficiaries' creditors generally cannot access assets held in the trust.

Trusts can also be useful in cases where business owners want to keep ownership control of the pharmacy but accrue future growth to family members. This can be accomplished by structuring ownership so that you or your holding company owns the voting shares while the trust owns the non-voting (growth) shares. Such an arrangement can create flexibility around the transfer of the business because it allows for planning the appropriate time to transfer shares of your company to your children in a manner that is commensurate with their role in the business.

That speaks to another potential use of trusts: managing your children. Most parents plan to pass their wealth to their kids, but if children realize their inheritance before they are mature enough to accept the responsibilities that come with wealth, the results can be problematic. Trusts can protect young heirs from the temptations associated with receiving large lump sums of capital. Specifically, trusts can be structured to pass on wealth when children reach a certain age or upon achieving certain milestones. In addition, they can be designed so that if the trustees are satisfied that the beneficiaries can handle the money themselves, the trust can be collapsed and the funds can be distributed to the beneficiaries.

Trusts can also be utilized to protect your estate assets in the event that you remarry or your surviving spouse remarries, so that the assets are not considered part of the new matrimonial property. Similarly, you can prevent the future spouses of your children from benefiting from your capital by placing assets in a family trust that stipulates that in the event of a divorce, the assets may be protected.

Finally, trusts can be extremely effective in philanthropy strategies. If you want to set money aside to benefit the community that has supported your pharmacy over the years, trusts can assist you in making a tax-efficient charitable donation. Charitable remainder trusts allow pharmacy owners to put cash, securities or real estate aside for philanthropy and then receive all the income from those assets while they are alive; upon death, the assets are transferred to the charity. When the trust is initially established, the value of the charity's residual interest is estimated by an actuary. This estimate triggers a tax receipt that can be put towards your income tax (provided the terms of the trust do not allow for capital encroachment). So if you are planning to give a donation to charity upon death, you can do so by utilizing a trust and thereby gain the tax benefits while you are still alive.

Gifting

Owning a pharmacy can be lucrative, and as pharmacist-owners begin to think about exiting their business or are in retirement, many quite fortunately find themselves in a position to gift money to their family, particularly their children. This is not just a matter of parental generosity. Tax savings are often one of the main reasons for owners to consider giving away some of their wealth while they are still alive. In some jurisdictions, there may be substantial value in gifting wealth before death and avoiding probate fees on assets that pass along from your estate. And many parents simply want to see their children enjoy the benefits of their wealth while they are still alive.

This understandable desire, however, raises several questions – ones to which your strategic wealth plan should provide answers. We can sum them up as: Who? Which assets? And how much?

In our experience, the thorniest question is usually "Who?" The answer can involve accounting for different circumstances and needs among your children, not to mention sometimes-complicated family dynamics. The reality is that a thoughtfully developed strategic wealth and succession plan might not mean that every family member receives an equal sum. For example, the gift to a child who has joined the family business might be lesser than the gift to a child who has not, because the strategic use of a corporate insurance policy for the first child offsets the difference. Or some owners might choose to gift asymmetrically simply because one child needs the money more than the other, or maybe they have children of their own where their sibling does not.

When it comes to which assets to transfer, remember that Canada has no gift tax, so you can give your children any amount of cash, and it will not be taxable as income or deductible as an expense. Giving away cash in your lifetime may save taxes against your estate after you die. Independent pharmacy owners may deploy a common strategy called an "estate freeze" (see the chapter on tax implications); other parents may prefer to give children cash to help them buy a home, fund their grandchildren's education, or ensure a child with a disability has enough to pay for a lifetime of needs. Establishing a trust for a child who is unable to manage money is a worthy consideration; a trust structure can provide parents with continued control of the assets while providing beneficiaries with money.

How much to gift early is a function of the purpose for the gift. Because it takes into account how much money you need to eventually retire and live at the level of comfort you desire, a strategic wealth plan will provide the basic framework of how much and when to transfer your wealth. Yet, just because you *can* transfer a certain amount of wealth to your kids does not mean you *should*. You might want to help your children but worry about giving too much too soon and creating a sense of entitlement. To paraphrase Warren Buffett: "Leave enough so that your kids can do something, but not so much that they can do nothing." Again, communication is vital. Talk to your kids about what they need or expect, and be sure to discuss with them the reasoning behind your giving plan.

Instilling a sense of stewardship of family assets should be an important goal, and educating children on how to handle money will provide them with a valuable skill set before they receive the majority of their inheritance. Parents may consider giving their children a small sum initially to determine how their kids handle the money. A good financial advisor should be prepared to assist you in preparing your children to become financially competent. (You should feel free to contact us if you require more information on this aspect.)

With wealth comes responsibility. Done the right way, transferring some wealth to your kids while you are still alive can be an effective way to teach them that lesson.

We've unpacked a lot of information in this chapter. Not all of it may be applicable in your case, and we therefore strongly recommend that you engage the expertise of a qualified tax planner and estate lawyer to integrate their advice with your financial plan.

CHAPTER 11:

Thinking Like an Investor

So you have sold your pharmacy business, and you feel prepared to get on with the next chapter of your life. You are now ready to reap the reward of all those years of hard work. See the pyramids. Spend time with your kids. Take that course you've always been interested in. Whatever you have long wanted to do but just didn't have the time for – well, now you do. Enjoy your retirement. You deserve it.

Now that the congratulations are out of the way, let's talk about the potential downside of your new reality. We do not wish to rain on anybody's parade, but the fact is that many pharmacist-owners – like a lot of entrepreneurs generally – struggle with retirement. Some feel they have lost their sense of purpose. Some have little idea about what to do with their time. Some feel disconnected from their community or their colleagues. It can be hard.

We are not saying at all that your retirement cannot indeed be true "golden years." A lot of the challenges are emotional and psychological, and it is natural to have some mixed emotions about leaving the life you knew behind. Give yourself time to get used to it. In all likelihood, you will get there soon enough.

There is, however, one particular area where you really do need to change the way you think about things: your approach to money. When you sell your business, you no longer have that dependable source of recurring revenue. You must now depend much more heavily than ever before on your assets. If you have realized a good return for your business, then those assets might be substantial. But however substantial they are, relying on them for your livelihood (and for your legacy) requires you to stop thinking like a business owner. Now, you must think like an investor.

Those are very different modes of thought because the world of running a pharmacy and the world of investing are very different beasts. For one thing, your income and your net worth as an investor are tied to the financial markets, over which you have no control. Just as importantly, you now must ensure that your source of retirement income will last a very long time. In Canada in 2019, a man who had made it to age 65 could expect to live, on average, for another 19.5 years, while the average woman at 65 had another 22.2 years ahead of her. At a minimum, then, your nest egg has to be managed to sustain you (and perhaps your spouse) for two decades, and quite probably longer, given continual advances in medicine.

This longevity challenge means that your priorities must shift from growing your capital (as you did when you owned your pharmacy business) to protecting your capital. It also means that you must plan for the long term – which in retirement is measured in decades, not years. People in general, let alone entrepreneurs, are often not wired to think this way. And many of the attitudes and habits that helped you build your business simply will not apply when allocating and preserving your capital in retirement.

1. The Investor Behaviour Penalty

For those reasons, getting support from a trusted and competent financial advisor is absolutely vital, in our opinion. Without it, you run a greater risk of squandering the opportunity the sale of your business has provided – a fate that befalls far too many former owners in retirement. (We refer you to Chapter 5 for some of the qualities and qualifications to look for in a financial advisor.) Advice, however, can only get you so far. At the end of the day, you are the master of your own fate as an investor. And the sad fact is that most investors do not do a very masterful job of managing their investments.

We only need to look at recent history to prove that assertion. In the mid-2000s, stock markets were going up, up and away as investors plowed money into equities that reached all-time highs – just as the Great Recession hit. After a terrible 2008, investors became despondent and pulled their money out of the market at a record pace. Capital inflows into mutual funds – a pretty good barometer of retail investor sentiment – plummeted. You don't need to guess what happened next: the market rebounded, delivering double-digit returns in 2010, and those despondent investors who gave up on equities missed out.

Want more evidence? Between 1994 and 2013, the average annual equity fund return was 8.7%. During the same period, the average annual return for investors in equity funds was 5.0%. That is a nearly four-percentage-point difference – and over time, it can really add up, thanks to the magic of compounding.

This difference, between what equities return and what equity investors earn, is often referred to as "the investor behaviour penalty" – because the reason it happens comes down to investor behaviour. To put it succinctly, most investors allocate capital (or withdraw capital from the market) at precisely the *wrong* time. By engaging in self-destructive behaviours, they have historically missed out on nearly half their potential return.

Over the long term, these behaviours can undermine your ability to build and maintain wealth. They can also turn your life in retirement into something of a rough experience, as your portfolio will be more subject than needed to the rollercoaster ride that markets can give investors in the short term.

2. Behavioural biases that can undermine wealth

If you as an investor have engaged in any of the behaviours we are going to discuss here, do not feel too bad. Neuroscience has proven that such responses are the result of millions of years of evolutionary adaptation; everyone is prone to them. The thing is, though, that capital markets are not exactly a natural construct, and the behaviours that might have served humans well 10,000 years ago often don't work very well for modern investors. In fact, quite the opposite.

What are some of the behaviours? Behavioural finance – the study of how psychological factors can affect market outcomes – has identified many biases and tendencies that can affect investors' decision-making. Our friend Joel Clark, the CEO of wealth management firm K.J. Harrison & Partners, likes to highlight three biases that are particularly relevant to retirement investing, and we thank him for letting us paraphrase his words of wisdom here:

Short-term bias

Humans are hard-wired to focus on the short term. It's just the way we are. Investors are no different. They tend to find the chance to realize short-term gains irresistibly attractive. Such "easy wins" stimulate the emotional centres of the brain that release dopamine – a neurochemical that makes us feel confident, positive and good about ourselves. (Pharmacists are well aware of this neurochemical as it forms part of their formal training.)

Yet while chasing short-term gains might make you feel better when you find one, the fact is that success in investing requires long-term discipline. Jumping in and out of allocations to realize short-term gains or avoid short-term pains is a recipe for lost long-term opportunities. Because of the way we are hard-wired, sitting out the market's ups-and-downs can be very difficult, but there is a real benefit to keeping a calm head while all about you are losing theirs.

If you had invested $10,000 in the S&P 500 in 1991 – and then proceeded to do *absolutely nothing* for 20 years, other than reinvesting the dividends – you would have had more than $200,000 by the end of 2020, representing a compound annual growth rate of 16.4%. And that's through 14 stock market corrections (when the S&P 500 index declined by 10% or more), three bear markets (declines of 20% or more) and the most severe economic downturn since the Great Depression.

In fact, since the Great Depression, stocks have generated positive returns over any given one-year period 74% of the time; over any given five-year period, they have delivered positive returns 93% of the time. So if history is any guide, staying the course and avoiding short-termism is a key element of investing success.

Yet, most investors do just the opposite. In the 1950s and 1960s, the average holding period for stocks was seven to eight years. Today, it is just 11 months.

As Warren Buffett once said, "The stock market is a device to transfer money from the 'impatient' to the 'patient.'"

Herd bias

Why can't we all get along? Well, most of us want to. As a rule, humans are highly social beings with a natural desire to be accepted by the group. In fact, the pain that arises from being socially excluded is felt in the same parts of the brain with which we feel actual physical pain. Psychologically, people tend to believe that a group makes better decisions than an individual does. In some cases, that might well be true, but not in all cases (as some might argue, the modern history of democracies clearly proves).

For investors, this innate bias makes it very hard to go against the herd – to be contrarian – even when logic and market conditions dictate. The herd bias makes it seem reasonable to jump into market bubbles just before they burst, or to abandon equities just when the stock market is about to recover from a correction.

Vividness bias

We humans learn from experience. We see the sun rise in the east every morning, and so we expect it to rise in the east tomorrow. (And yes, humans figured that out before astronomers figured out the rotation of the earth.) That extrapolation has yet to be proven wrong. Still, our tendency to project the immediate past into the distant future applies in other areas of life, too, and not always to our benefit.

As Warren Buffett has pointed out, we tend to discount the likelihood of low-probability events occurring when they haven't occurred recently, and we tend to overvalue their likelihood when they have occurred recently. If you had asked most people in 2019 about the likelihood of a global pandemic killing hundreds of thousands and shutting down the global economy within the next 10 years, they no doubt would have found that prospect highly unlikely; after all, such a disaster had not occurred since the Spanish Flu epidemic of a hundred years before. Ask the same question today, and you might get a very different answer.

The point is not whether people's expectations turn out to be right or wrong, but that they are based on the demonstrably false premise that what just happened is more likely to occur in the future *because* it just happened, and what hasn't happened recently is less likely to occur in the future *because* it hasn't happened in a while. That's vividness bias.

In the world of investing, an overvaluation of recent results can lead investors to believe those results will continue in the future. Vividness bias makes them think a stock price that has been soaring will continue to soar, or that a stock that has been falling will continue to fall. This is analogous to driving by looking in the rear-view mirror instead of through the front windshield.

3. Overcoming your biases

Investors are people, and as people, their emotions, biases and assumptions can get in the way of investing success. So how can you overcome these failings and avoid the behaviours that can undermine their long-term wealth?

In our view, the first and most crucial step is to have a strategic wealth plan that defines financial success and aligns capital allocation decisions to your personal goals and objectives. A plan can help give you the discipline to "keep your eye on the prize" and not be distracted by short-term opportunities or risks. It allows you to target an appropriate return for your portfolio while defining the amount of risk you are willing to assume. Yes, you could chase high-risk opportunities in hopes of realizing high returns, but a strategic wealth plan will remind you that you might not need to.

Aligning investments to your goals is key to smart capital allocation within your portfolio, and those goals will have different priorities. Let's look at how that might work in practice.

- In retirement, you will probably want to keep a certain portion of your assets available for emergencies. You can't afford to lose it, and it needs to be highly liquid. So it might make sense to allocate this portion of your portfolio into low – or no-risk instruments, such as gold, cash or insurance, even though their nominal rate of return is zero.

- Next on the priority ranking would be meeting essential lifestyle requirements, like your house and healthcare expenses. You can probably afford to take on some risk in this area and generate some return, but you need to keep this portion of your portfolio safe – everyone has to pay their bills. So an allocation to short-term bonds or other fixed-income instruments might be worth considering.

- After essential lifestyle expenses come non-essential expenses – the fun stuff, like travel and entertainment. You can afford to take on more risk here in hopes of higher returns, so diversified growth assets, such as a diversified portfolio of equities, may be a suitable allocation.

- Finally, there are those assets you are setting aside for your legacy, which by definition you can live without. Here, taking on substantive risk and seeking higher returns might make sense, so an aggressive growth portfolio might be the best allocation.

In summary, avoiding investing biases entails ensuring that your investments line up with your retirement goals. That is why a sound wealth plan is *strategic*. When it comes to investing, emotion is rarely your friend.

Nine Final Thoughts on Investing

1. The skills you used to build your pharmacy business are very different from the skills you will require to safely invest your nest egg.

2. As you transition from pharmacy business owner to investor, your historical source of steady income and wealth creation will be replaced with aperiodic returns provided by financial assets.

3. Understanding the relationship between risk and return is paramount to investing.

4. Avoid placing yourself on an emotional investment roller-coaster in order to avoid capitulation at the wrong time.

5. Part of the secret sauce of long-term investment returns is to avoid big drawdowns during market rollovers and corrections.

6. Stocks and bonds asset allocation requires supplementation with alternative investment classes to moderate market volatility and returns.

7. Too much conflicting information! The democratization of marketing information continues to provide confusing and often contradictory signals.

8. The financial services industry is always in a "sell" mode to convince investors to buy their products regardless of whether it is in your best interests.

9. Retaining a discretionary financial advisor can free you from the day-to-day decision-making and energy required to attain a risk-adjusted return on your investment portfolio.

Addendum

Having finished what we thought was the final draft of this book, we unearthed a couple other relevant subjects – such is the curse of knowing so much! In this section, we discuss the strategic use of insurance in estate planning and a few need-to-knows about shareholder agreements. These are areas that can have significant applications when it comes to selling your pharmacy business, yet they might reasonably be considered "nice-to-haves" rather than "must-haves" in your business exit knowledge toolkit. So we felt that they were best suited as an addendum.

The strategic use of insurance

The goal of estate planning is to ensure that the assets of an individual or family are distributed according to their wishes after death. Life insurance is often used as a solution to problems and needs identified in the estate planning process. Below, we outline three estate planning strategies that include life insurance: estate preservation, estate equalization and business succession planning.

Estate Preservation

Life insurance can assist with estate preservation. Assume that pharmacy owners Ed and his spouse Cheryl have an estate worth $3 million. Part of the estate planning process would include determining the liabilities of their estate upon death. Income taxes, estate administration taxes (commonly known as probate fees), capital gain taxes and creditors can all eat away at an otherwise sizable estate.

The Income Tax Act deems that every capital asset a person owns – an investment portfolio, real property, the family pharmacy business, and so on – is deemed to be sold at fair market value the day before the person dies. With a few exceptions, like one's principal residence, half of any gain in value on this deemed sale is subject to tax. Probate fees apply to any asset that does not pass to an heir outside of the estate.

If planning is not done in advance, Ed and Cheryl's estate will likely be worth far less than $3 million upon death. In some situations, it becomes necessary for the estate executors to sell assets that the family does not want sold, like the cherished family cottage, because there is not enough cash in the estate to pay liabilities. Some assets, including certain types of commercial property and shares in private companies (like pharmacies), do not always have ready buyers and might have to be sold for less than the desired value. This is the dreaded "fire sale" scenario. (For simplicity and where applicable, we will ignore regulatory restrictions placed on pharmacy ownership imposed by provincial self-regulating bodies.)

Life insurance can be used to cover the anticipated estate liabilities, preserve the estate at the $3 million level and ensure that assets the family wants to keep do not have to be sold. The proceeds of a life insurance policy are paid out tax-free, and probate fees can also be avoided if a named beneficiary is used. Estate planning will also determine whose life should be insured. The Income Tax Act permits a rollover at the deceased person's adjusted cost base of capital assets bequeathed to a spouse and all of the capital gains tax on those assets will only be payable when the spouse sells or transfers the property (or is deemed to upon their death). If capital gains tax is the biggest concern for the estate, and if the spousal rollover will be available for a large portion of the capital assets, then joint last-to-die insurance might be the best choice. The death benefit will then be paid when the money is most needed: upon the death of the second spouse. This type of insurance has the advantage of being much less expensive than a policy on the life of one spouse.

Estate Equalization

Life insurance can also be used for estate equalization. Assume that Ed and Cheryl have two children, Alice and Christopher, whom they wish to treat equally, or at least fairly. If all of the estate is in cash, or can easily be turned into cash, then $1.5 million each is the obvious split of the $3 million estate. But this is rarely the case. Even if $2 million of the value is in the shares of a private family pharmacy business, $500,000 in the family cottage and $500,000 in liquid assets, many people simply leave their assets equally to their children. This can be a terrible mistake and often not practical, especially if neither child is a pharmacist or only one is a licensed pharmacy practitioner.

First, consider the family pharmacy business. What if Alice works in the family business as the staff pharmacist and Christopher is a dentist? To state it plainly, it is often a disaster leading to the demise of the business to leave the shares of a private business to heirs who do not work in the business. It is also unrealistic to assume that family members will not fight over control of assets. When it comes to property such as the family cottage, parents might be surprised when they ask who wants to inherit it (with the attendant cost and effort of future upkeep). Yes, the children should be asked! In fact, family meetings (which should be held as part of the estate planning process, especially when family businesses are involved or the estates are otherwise complex) are in our view the most important part of the entire process.

It may be the case that Alice continues to use the cottage extensively but Christopher stopped visiting a few years ago, so the decision is made to leave Alice the shares of the family pharmacy business and the family cottage. We have just given her $2.5 million of the $3 million estate! The most effective way to equalize the estate (and normally the only way to do it in the short run) is to buy an insurance policy naming Christopher as the beneficiary. But is it necessary to buy a policy to cover the full $2 million shortfall? The aim should be fairness and not necessarily dollar-for-dollar equality. Given that the shares of a private pharmacy business may be hard to sell and assuming that Alice is a big part of the reason that the business is currently worth $2 million rather than less, perhaps Ed and Cheryl decide that a $2 million insurance policy – in other words, $2 million in cash rather than shares of a private company – is sufficient to treat Christopher fairly. In the end, what is fair is a subjective decision.

Whenever a large asset is being left to one heir to the exclusion of others, life insurance can be used to make the estate equal or fair for everyone.

Business Succession Planning

What is the relationship between business succession planning and estate planning? To the extent that the business is being passed on at death, business succession planning can be viewed as part of estate planning. But obviously a business can be sold or transferred before death, in which case business succession planning is a separate process. A pharmacy business owner generally has three options when it comes to business succession: transfer the business to family members, sell to employees or partners, or sell to a third party. All three can occur before death or at death.

If the pharmacy business is owned by more than one individual or family, it is common to have a "buy/sell" agreement between the business owners. Let's continue with the family we discussed above. Assume that Ed Smith owns the business with Harry Jones. A buy/sell agreement would stipulate that if Harry dies, Ed will buy Harry's shares and vice versa. There are several ways to structure these arrangements. The shares can be bought personally by the surviving shareholder or there can be an agreement that the corporation will redeem the shares of the deceased shareholder. Consideration must also be given to utilizing the capital gains exemption of each shareholder.

Whatever structure is chosen, one of the most important planning points is to secure the source of the funds for the buyout. Putting a formal agreement in place does not mean much if you cannot be sure that you or your business partner will have the funds available for the buyout when the time comes. Life insurance is the most certain and effective way to ensure that the funds will be available when they are needed.

The proceeds of a life insurance policy are paid to a corporation tax-free. But many people, including many business owners, do not realize that the proceeds of the policy can also flow out of the corporation to shareholders tax-free (or very close to it) through the Capital Dividend Account. This affords opportunities for tax planning. A very common strategy (whether in the context of a buy/sell agreement or not) is to use the Capital Dividend Account to redeem the shares of a shareholder upon death. This can lead to a significant reduction, and sometimes a complete elimination, of taxes.

An estate freeze is a common planning strategy used by business owners. In our example, Ed might undertake an estate freeze for the business. On a tax-deferred rollover basis, he transfers all of his common shares to a holding company and takes back voting preferred shares that pay regular dividends and allow him to keep control of the company. Common shares of the company would then be issued to his daughter Alice for a nominal value. This strategy "freezes" the value of Ed's capital gain and the future growth in the company will be reflected in the common shares held by Alice. If Ed is not yet completely sure who will take over the business, it is common to have a discretionary family trust subscribe for the common shares. This trust could list Ed's wife Cheryl and their children as beneficiaries. This does not mean that the company shares will necessarily end up in the hands of all of the beneficiaries. Because it is a discretionary trust, the decision to flow all of the shares of the company to Alice can be made at a later point.

The shareholder agreement

When we meet with pharmacy owners, we often see situations where partners in a pharmacy business could benefit from developing a comprehensive shareholder agreement – a contract between shareholders of an incorporated business that puts mechanisms in place to deal with important issues with a view to avoiding problems in the future.

It does so by providing a mechanism for setting out the principles to protect the interests of all the shareholders in the event of changing circumstances. Specifically, a shareholders' agreement contains the rights and obligations of shareholders of a company addressing matters related to governing its management and structure, initial and continued funding, and its administration and business activities.

While it is not a legal requirement for a company to have a shareholder agreement, pharmacy owners today are well advised to adopt one as part of the establishment of a pharmacy ownership relationship.

Such an agreement commonly includes policies governing the following matters:

- Company structure, including the composition of the capital of the company and its internal rules.

- Appointment of directors, including the power of each shareholder to appoint a director or directors, and the authority of such directors when making decisions.

- Management of the company and directing the company management to prepare financial and management reports for the shareholders, all in accordance with generally accepted accounting principles applicable at the time.

- Restrictions on the transfer of shares, including a provision that if one shareholder dies or wishes to sell their shares in the company, the other shareholder has the first option, on certain terms, to purchase the shares. There may be other provisions prohibiting the transfer of shares, except in certain circumstances, as well as a mechanism to determine a fair value for the shares.

- Dividends and the provision of additional funding by the shareholders, including the methods and the proportions in which the shareholders will provide funds to maintain the company, the amount of the profits to be allocated as dividends each year, and a procedure for resolving disputes that arise in respect of these matters.

- A "buy-and-sell" clause (shotgun) in the event shareholders can no longer harmoniously remain shareholders.

- Provisions for key-person insurance in the event of the untimely death of a shareholder.

- The rights of shareholders and directors, including access to records and any variations or additions to the statutory powers, rights and duties of shareholders and directors.

- A dispute resolution mechanism, such as a provision dealing in matters which could lead to substantial injury to the company as a going concern, and which seem incapable of satisfactory long-term resolution by mediation or negotiation.

- Non-competition provisions to prevent either shareholder from setting up a pharmacy business in competition to the company within a prescribed time period and geographical distance from the existing pharmacy.

- Confidentiality provisions relating to exposure of company documents, both during the period of the shareholder agreement and following the termination of the agreement.

- Duties of the shareholders with regard to the company and each other in the event of the company being liquidated.

In conclusion, a shareholder agreement is a valuable safeguard, providing a procedural framework to govern the internal management of a company that owns your pharmacy. It is particularly useful in cases where there is no clear majority shareholder in your business and as such minimizes the potential for disputes that can detrimentally affect the company.